# THE PACIFIC GARDEN MISSION
## A Doorway to Heaven

# The Pacific Garden Mission

## A DOORWAY TO HEAVEN

BY

## Carl F. H. Henry

INTRODUCTION
By H. A. Ironside. Litt.D.

EIGHTH EDITION

## ZONDERVAN PUBLISHING HOUSE
### GRAND RAPIDS, MICHIGAN

THE PACIFIC GARDEN MISSION
Copyright 1942 by
Zondervan Publishing House
Grand Rapids, Michigan

*Printed in the United States of America*

DEDICATED TO
Long Island's "Mother Christy,"
who first pleaded with the author
to receive Christ as Savior

# INTRODUCTION

Those who have decided that the age of miracles has long gone by will do well to read and ponder over this amazing record of sixty-five years of Mission history, in a great city and in the midst of its very worst section morally. That the Gospel of Christ has lost nothing of its old-time virility but that it is still the dynamic of God unto salvation to every one that believeth is here proven to a demonstration. In a masterly way the gifted author has presented a panorama of regeneration—a moving picture of the redeeming value of the blood of Christ and the life-giving energy of the Holy Spirit, manifested in the salvaging of human wreckage and the new creation of utterly lost men and women,—transforming drunkards, gamblers and criminals of all types into devoted saints of God and hard-toiling servants of the Lord of glory, whose delight is to seek to bring others to know Him who has wrought so mightily on their own behalf.

If the Pacific Garden Mission had been the spiritual birth-place of only a few outstanding converts such as Harry Monroe, Billy Sunday, Melvin A. Trotter, Edward Cord, Bill Hadley and Walter McDonald, it would be worth all the money and labor expended through the two-thirds of a century of its existence. But here we read of scores of degraded sinners transformed into conscientious and upright children of God, through the miracle of the new birth which alone enables one to enter into and enjoy the blessedness of the Kingdom of God.

For more than thirty years it has been my own privilege to drop into the Mission occasionally, to be thrilled by the testimonies of its happy converts whose joy in their deliverance from the bondage of sin often beggars all description. It was in the old days, years ago, before the railways merged and took over all the express companies that I heard an old man with a shining face exclaim, "My friends, Wells Fargo and Company's Express couldn't have expressed my feelings the night God saved me and the load of guilt and sin was lifted from my heart." It was oddly put, but the reality of a great deliverance from a terrible thralldom was behind it all. And this has been true, and is true today, of hundreds, yes thousands, who have knelt at the old fashioned mourner's bench or penitent-form at the "altar" of the

Pacific Garden Mission and there met the Eternal One who says, "Look unto me and be ye saved, for I am God and there is none else." Revealed in Christ Jesus, whose name means literally Jehovah the Savior, He has manifested His deep personal interest in all who bow before Him in repentance and call upon Him in faith.

This book is the best answer to the specious sophestries and, as some think conclusive arguments, of infidelity and atheism I have ever seen. These men know there is a God for they called upon Him and He responded to their cry. Like the once-blind man of whom we read in John 9, they exclaim as with one voice, "Whereas once I was blind now I see." And they know that no power but that of God could ever have wrought so great a change.

It is safe to say that no perversion of the gospel such as that offered in modernistic pulpits today could ever effect such transformations as we read of here. In the Pacific Garden Mission there has been no place through all the years of its existence for any other than the old-fashioned preaching of the three R's— Ruin, Redemption and Regeneration. Its preachers and converts alike could ever sing

"I have no other argument,
I want no other plea,
It is enough that Jesus died
And that He died for me."

This gospel demonstrates its divine origin and its inspired character by what it does. Paul could say, "I am not ashamed of the gospel of Christ for it is the power of God unto salvation to every one that believeth . . . for therein is the righteousness of God revealed from faith to faith as it is written, The just shall live by faith" (Romans 1:16, 17). In the evangelical churches and missions everywhere the proof of this is evidenced, and this has been specially true in the record of these years of testimony for Christ of the Pacific Garden Mission, and the effectiveness of the many evangelists who were there brought to know Him whom to know is life eternal. Saved themselves, many of them have gone forth through the length and breadth of this and other lands carrying the same message to uncounted millions and leading vast numbers to the Saviour who met them in their hopelessness and wretchedness and revealed Himself to them as the Almighty Deliverer. These men were themselves exemplifications of the Great Physician's power to heal sin-sick souls, to renew blighted lives, to bind up broken hearts and to lift from the lowest depths of despair to the highest heights of blessing. The story of this Mission and its converts is a new chapter in the Acts of the Holy Spirit proving that Jesus Christ is indeed the same yesterday, today, and forever.

No one who is even slightly familiar with the work and testimony of the Pacific Garden Mission will question the accuracy of the story here set forth. Rather, he will exclaim with Sheba's queen, "The half hath not been told." It would not be possible to inscribe in a book the greatest triumphs of this work, for they are of so sacred a character that human language could not portray or express them aright. They are among those spiritual things which are spiritually discerned. If all the details of those sixty-five years were to be put down on paper, so far as it is possible to describe them, it would take more than the Library of Congress to house the books that would have to be written. Only eternity will reveal all that the work of Col. and Mrs. Clarke and their successors has meant to poor sin-laden humanity for whom Christ died.

Nor were these poor derelicts the only ones benefited by contact with this great work. Some of the ablest preachers and teachers of the Word were trained to a large extent in the Pacific Garden Mission. Perhaps there is no greater expounder of Scripture in America than Dr. William Evans, who is internationally known and whose messages have been blessed to thousands in this and many other lands. As a student of the Moody Bible Institute, young Evans led the singing and played a cornet at the Mission and later served for two years as an assistant to Harry Monroe. He counts the time spent in that work as part of the schooling that fitted him for his later worldwide ministry.

It has been my privilege to know many of those mentioned in this volume. I have seen the grace of God leading them on in Christ's triumph. I have recognized their lowly, self-sacrificing interest in others who are still where they once were. I have noted their dependence on God, and have been moved by their simplicity as they went to Him in prayer, believing He meant what He said when He bade them be not anxious about anything, but in everything by prayer and supplication with thanksgiving make known their requests. And I know they were upheld by the Hand of Omnipotence which they grasped in faith as they knelt at the cross. Their's has been a real salvation from real sin and wickedness.

But I must not attempt to hold anyone longer at the door. Open and enter in and see for yourself this great galaxy of those who have surrendered to the cross of Christ. And as you move on through these stirring chapters you will find yourself exclaiming with awe and reverence "What hath God wrought!"

H. A. IRONSIDE, Litt. D.

# PREFACE

It is surprising indeed how God has blessed this brief testimony to the power of the Gospel. Yet the more one walks with Christ, the less one marvels at the hold which the story of redemption takes upon the minds and hearts of men. One cannot company with Him without expecting miracles to happen.

This humble effort is a narrative footnote to the procession of twice-born men that stretches back across the centuries to the entrance of Christ into the stream of humanity. The redeeming power that made a new creature of Paul of Tarsus, Justin Martyr, Augustine and others, who had first turned in vain to Christless philosophies, is still alone able completely to change men's lives. Pacific Garden Mission is one of a multitude of centers where this saving grace is uncompromisingly proclaimed.

The old mission, meeting place of two worlds, is replete with surprises for all who come. For sixty-seven years prospective saints have been snatched from the brink of hell. Today evangelists, pastors, mission workers and Christian laymen by the thousands trace their first impulse to surrender their lives to Christ to this mission. More than thirty thousand converts have found Jesus Christ in the shadow of this sanctuary. Now they are respectable members of the business and social world; the degradation and destitution of earlier years is but a reminder of the subsequent grace of God.

The record of this mission, oldest in the northwest and second oldest in the nation, for reclaiming the humanly incorrigible, makes a factual epic more thrilling than any of the world's fancies.

CARL F. H. HENRY

# TABLE OF CONTENTS

| CHAPTER | | PAGE |
|---|---|---|
| I. | DOORWAYS TO HEAVEN AND HELL | 13 |
| II. | GOD'S FLOPHOUSE | 19 |
| III. | THE ANGEL OF THE SLUMS | 25 |
| IV. | THE SHIFT TO PACIFIC BEER GARDEN | 29 |
| V. | FROM COUNTERFEITING TO REALITY | 37 |
| VI. | LOADING THE BASES ON THE SAWDUST TRAIL | 41 |
| VII. | MEL TROTTER'S SUICIDE NIGHT | 47 |
| VIII. | A CRADLE OF AMERICAN EVANGELISM | 51 |
| IX. | THE GREAT TRIUMVIRATE | 64 |
| X. | IN THE SHADOW OF THE MISSION MOTHER | 79 |
| XI. | A TWENTIETH-CENTURY JONAH | 88 |
| XII. | FIVE FEET FIVE INCHES OF SNOW | 92 |
| XIII. | PORT OF MISSING MEN | 98 |
| XIV. | CALVARY COVERS IT ALL | 103 |
| XV. | A BOX SEAT ON "MURDERER'S ROW" | 111 |
| XVI. | RELICS OF THE PAST | 116 |
| XVII. | THE APOSTLE OF STATE STREET | 120 |
| XVIII. | THE MAN WHO HEARD GOD LAUGH | 127 |
| XIX. | TRIMMING THE LOWER LIGHTS | 130 |
| XX. | FOLD OF THE LOST SHEEP | 136 |

# CHAPTER I

## DOORWAYS TO HEAVEN AND HELL

Chicago's Loop, like the heart of any huge city, is three steps from heaven and two steps from hell.

It was a bristling evening in May. Rough and ready, clad in old clothes like any man of the streets, I wandered aimlessly through the Loop. Into the shifting eyes of down-and-outers who sauntered by, I looked with conscious effort to feel the emotions of men whose feelings are jaded, and to think the thoughts of men too tired to think.

It was no easy job, this business of a preacher being a bum, even for a night or two.

Colorless, empty, bleary eyes. Heavy, lazy, tired feet. Workers, homeward bound, after a day's work. Businessmen hurrying to a cab or to the elevated. Homeless outcasts. Wandering refugees. Drink and drug addicts. Philanthropist and harlot, millionaire and stenographer walking the same streets.

From Madison, I shuffled southward on State street, banked on either side by the shopping district that brings throngs to showrooms and counters. There was Kresge's, Walgreen's, Grant's, and, as I neared Adams, the rear annex of the famed Palmer House, and then the Fair. Newsstands, traffic lights and street corners were passed with monotonous succession, as also the unending chain of stores: Woolworth's, Howard's, Benson and Rixon's, Hilton's, the Hub, and then Jackson boulevard; Rothschild's, Goldblatt Brothers, and then Van Buren street with the elevated circuit that encloses the Loop. Just inside that circuit, as night fell, glittered the flickering lights of the Rialto, heralding a giant stage revue, the world's greatest show, and, as a Saturday night special at 12:05, "Paris in Chicago."

Those words were the first tangible evidence that State street's "500 block" was just ahead. City within a city, it is the fair ground of burlesque and 30-cent a night hotels, pawn shops and women barbers, bar-rooms and cut-rate stores, gloomy dens and greasy lunch counters that still feature a hot dog or a hamburger on a bun for a nickel. Just one step

13

from the Loop, and opposite the modern Sears' department store which extends a block long from Van Buren to Congress, flows this weird mixture of two worlds. White men, black men, yellow men surge in and out of the changing crowds. The best of men and the worst of men, the best of women and the worst of women are there. Strangers hurry through the throngs to the Dearborn-Polk Street Station for trains to eastern Canada and the southwest, unaware that plain clothes detectives patrol the streets.

Here young couples wander and old men shuffle into burlesque houses, lured inside by strip tease billboards displaying immodest women. Down State street walks a stunningly dressed butterfly, with a graceful rhythm and an inviting air. Not until she turns into the burlesque house for the nightly performances is it apparent that expert facial decoration has sheared ten or fifteen years from the world view, but not from the heart.

Outside the customers slide their two dimes through the ticket window to the gray-haired woman cashier and then trickle inside. At the State-Harrison, beautiful Ann Corio furnishes the week's attraction in "Swamp Woman," with "Guilty Parents" scheduled for an early appearance. Every Saturday night promises a midnight show. The lurid display signs of two other burlesque houses scream their features. "Unknown Blonde" is the attraction at one of them, and a taxicab arrives there with three girls and two sailors. State street is broken up with subway construction, so the pride of the navy convoys its cargo to the sidewalk pickaback. The crowd chuckles.

All the way from Russell's Silver Bar at State and Van Buren to the State-Harrison Bar, the "500 block" is a seminary of sin with a sprinkling of ordinary businesses. Beyond Russell's corner spot stands one of the omnipresent Thompson restaurants. Then the first "loan bank," probably so dubbed to impress the paupers visiting the pawn shop that there isn't so much sting in poverty after all, flaunts its welcome. Next comes the first "hotel," with rooms as low as thirty-five cents. Between two men's clothing shops—one with 15-cent neckties in the show window and the other modestly affirming itself the "largest retailers of pants in America"—stands Bradley's Bar.

Just beyond another jewelry pawn shop vibrates the tumultuous jazz echo of the Club Cabana, with its red and green

lights over the street windows, but no yellow for caution.
A casual glance through the tilted blinds reveals that the
crowd is merry and business is good, to desecrate the ad-
jective.

Next is a game shop and lunch counter, where patrons
munch a sandwich and gulp down a cup of coffee between
target practice on wooden ducks and other mechanical con-
tests, some of which call for skill and others for luck, but all
of which require nickels, dimes and quarters. Still pictures
of nude women for a penny a series and movie pictures of
artists' models for a nickel a run pack in the small change.
A roly-poly colored boy, almost as wide as tall, runs back and
forth between the penny arcade and the street window of the
nearby Pink Poodle, a night club featuring "Puppets on
Parade." He presses his nose flat against the window,
watches the dancer do her rhumba, mutters "She's not so hot,
even if she thinks she is," and goes back to spend another
penny.

Beyond the arcade are two more pawn shops and between
them, with its hilarity concealed from the street world by
super-decorated windows, Millie's. Then comes another cheap
hotel—rooms at thirty cents—and the Babette, where liquor
flows freely. Next door is the thirty-cent Gem, first of the
three slapstick burlesque houses as one walks south in this
block. Street signs display half-naked women, and whatever
sensuous appeal the photographers and artists have overlooked
has been more than offset by sign-writers who spare no super-
latives to evoke trade. The ticket girl is unattractive and the
barker, whose appearance fits him nicely into the regular
society of the "500 block," mumbles his announcements just
unintelligibly enough to arouse the question whether he is
deliberately attempting to evade being understood.

With mingled speeds the throng moves in all directions.
The collection of human faces changes every few seconds,
but it is none the less interesting. Old men and old women,
mostly alone, sometimes in couples, bend over the street as
they plod along. Middle-aged men and middle-aged women,
their foreheads deeply lined with furrows, follow the path of
least resistance through the crowd. Young people, some
jolly, some tired, wind in and out, in search of a good time.
Now and then they dart into a tavern, or into a recreation
parlor, and then out into the streets again. Soldiers and sail-

ors walk along leisurely; the nation is at war and this is their leave. They come with buddies, soldier with soldier and sailor with sailor, and sometimes they have found giggling companions for the night. Despite the early evening hour, men are already swaying on the streets like trees bending with the wind.

From across the street echo strange words and music for a land like this. A street meeting is in progress and a Chicago Tract Society group is singing "Wonderful Words of Life." The theme comes with shocking suddenness to those who live intensely in the "500 block" without any life at all. Almost everything is peddled within hearing distance: liquor, dope, women.

A few hags—middle-aged women, unattractive despite layers of rouge—ply their trade as street walkers. Their story is more disgusting than that of the younger prostitutes for whom promoters, procurers and madams, not to mention taxi drivers and bellhops, discover prospects. Most any police station can tell the story of the prostitutes who pay occasional penalty in court, but not much is done about the operators who profit from the business, and who select the "right girls" to make a honky-tonk a popular resort. The policeman's say-so sends a prostitute to jail for three to six months, but nobody gets the so-called "barrel of evidence" necessary to land a solicitor, madam, owner or promoter.

Most of these younger girls are neither professional nor successful prostitutes. They did not set up a girlhood ambition for venal lewdness. They became commercial prostitutes before they reached the decision. From a job as waitress in a low-class drinking joint they found it easy to make a few dollars occasionally while on dates with "nice fellows." Then, confronted with an illegitimate child, or with sex delinquency for which neither psychiatric nor medical treatment is being provided, or beset with an impassioned desire for drugs and the necessity for money, they suddenly find themselves commercial prostitutes. Some of them even enjoy their association with small-time rackets and racketeers, which brings extra prominence. But few of them find prostitution so financially profitable that they engage a selected clientele; such girls are not found in the brothels and hovels of the slum districts. These are not the "hostess for a night" professionals for which some hotels have become infamous. but they are the low-grade, low-priced, unsuccessful prostitutes who are the greatest venereal disease menace. Their solicitors, clever middle-aged men who know how to overlook curious folks that obviously want to be solicited, know the poolrooms and dubious resorts where they can pick up delinquent youngsters.

There aren't many red lights in the State street area now, and the number of prostitutes is smaller. The most obvious reason is that there aren't as many prospects this year. There are fewer drifters and less men out of work, because these are war years, and the armed forces and defense plants have put all available hands behind triggers and machines. So the prostitutes, too, have been on the move to defense centers and other areas where lonely men are susceptible to commercially exploited women and girls.

Beyond the burlesque house is the entrance to the Yes-Yes Club, and then another pawn shop. Then, on the door of the Kelly Building is posted this rather curious announcement for war-time: "U. S. Army Moved to 515 S. Franklin." Along the sidewalks are display signs, inviting young men to join the Army or the Marines for a broader education.

Shoe store, pawn shop, radio store, Regal Hotel and thirty-five cent rooms, and so it goes. The Pink Poodle features an all-star girl revue, and a passing glance through the blinds shows the bar lined with drinkers; toward the rear a mint-gold blonde dancer, garbed in black satin on a ration plan, lithely moves in step to semi-savage rhythm. She finishes her number and then an older performer, jet hair hanging over her orchid gown, steps into the spotlight for a whirl of dance steps. The glassy-eyed cashier sits at his register with a stare, undisturbed except by customers on their way in or out.

Radio shop, a recreation center with mechanical games, a lunch bar with five-cent hamburgers, pawn shop, another lunch counter, and then the Eagle Hotel with thirty-cent rooms. A men's clothing store. Then the Gay 90's Arcade, a playland with games, penny film machines, and special tattooing service that includes names of sweethearts, special designs, or one's social security number. Another pawn shop. Then the Tiny Spot, and next door, another burlesque theatre —for adults only. Another lunch room, from the rear of which echoes the click of colliding billiard balls. Then Moore's Hotel—rooms fifty cents and up. Then a uniform

supply house, with outfits for all comers, whether for the
restaurant waiter or the rodeo cowboy. Next, pawn shop
number nine in the same block, same side of the street. Next
door, the State-Harrison burlesque, with a large signboard
blazing forth the question, "What's Wrong With Love?"
Then, at the corner, the State-Harrison grill and bar, and the
fat man who sits on a box and shouts, "Chicago Tribune!"

Sex, liquor, poverty and squalor tell the story of most of
that block from the Silver Bar to the State-Harrison burlesque
with "beautiful Ann Corio." Women without morals at
twenty cents a ticket for the show. Whiskey at fifty cents a
half-pint. A meal for seventeen cents: hamburger steak, dessert and coffee. Across the street it is the same story. The
Trocadero Club, cut-rate stores, a book store with pamphlets
on magic, astrology and dreams.

Beyond the glittering lights of the "500 block" and the
Harrison intersection flicker the darkening recesses of south
State. The light may be dimmer, but the "600 block" tells
the same story. Cigar store, pawn broker, restaurant, movie
house featuring a screen show and burlesque for fifteen cents,
pawn shop, the Red Hot Burlesque located at the new State-Harrison subway entrance, the New Paris Theatre, a tatooing
studio, a lunch counter and billiard room, the Fleetwood Hotel
—not for men only—with rooms at sixty cents, a restaurant,
a barber shop with three lady barbers wearing white satin
aprons, the Elk Hotel—for men only—with rooms as low as
thirty cents a day, a restaurant, another game and recreation
center, and then the strangest doorway on all south State
street . . . . . the doorway to heaven.

## Chapter II

## GOD'S FLOPHOUSE

Stained with blood and seared with lust, sinners have thronged to the Pacific Garden Mission no less than to the other strange hangouts in this block. For twenty years it has been the only church in "The Street of Harlots."

Founded in 1877, it is the oldest rescue mission in the Northwest, the second oldest in America, and probably the best known in the world. It has not been closed a night since its beginnings.

Bank presidents, lawyers, farmers, sailors, ex-convicts and tramps have visited there, some out of desperate need and others out of mere curiosity, but all have been spiritually lifted. Billy Sunday was a nationally-known baseball player when he walked in; when he left he was destined to become one of the most famous evangelists in Christian revivalism. Mel Trotter was a candidate for suicide in Lake Michigan when he stopped; he went out a firebrand for God's kingdom.

Here, on "Bum Boulevard"—another name for this stretch of Chicago's world-famous State street—the driftwood of humanity floats in. Once wealthy men from fine families, who have lost themselves and their loved ones, come for respite for their tortured souls. Here they learn that sin pays off in broken hearts, broken minds, broken families and purses, yet there is no sorrow that heaven cannot heal, and it is not yet too late to find the long-sought glory and sparkle of life.

Suspended outside the second story, shaped like a cross ten feet long and more than half as wide, glows a red neon sign: JESUS SAVES. The warm letters reach the eye almost simultaneously with the ear's throb to the loud speaker which carries the mission service to the street. Old hymns echo through the night air, and the keen thrusts of the speakers pierce every needy heart within hearing distance.

Nobody walks past the familiar eighteen-foot neon sign PACIFIC GARDEN MISSION and the additional reminder MOTHER'S PRAYERS HAVE FOLLOWED YOU, without a personal worker's invitation to attend the service and without receiving a Gospel tract, unless it is rejected. "Four Things God Wants You

19

To Know," and other folders go into many thousands of pockets and homes weekly.

Any night at 7:45 will find a crowd many times the size of most prayer meetings and much more ready to confess its need. Homeless men in ragged overcoats or sweaters sit with bent heads on rough, wooden chairs. Some seem to be praying, some half listening to the gospel music and preaching; others are too tired either to pray, listen or sleep. Their thoughts may be on the "good supper" they'll get downstairs after the service, but the preacher shouts and repeats that there is always hunger without the Bread of Life. It takes untold perspiration to arouse in these men the guilt of rejecting Christ, the need of repentance and faith in His Saviorhood.

During World War II attendance has hovered at one hundred every week-night, a considerable decrease. Men otherwise not close to the government's heart become suddenly important in the trenches and in industry. But Pacific Garden Mission, for almost 24,000 nights in peace and in war time, has stressed the individual's eternal worth in God's sight, and a congregation aggregating more than two million has heard the call, "Come to Jesus."

There is an underlying routine—song service led by a visiting group, testimonies, special music numbers, the Gospel message, the invitation to take Christ as Savior—but almost anything may happen to change the program. The only invariable feature is the closing appeal; for sixty-five years it has been given, and the mission intends thus to continue every night in every year until the age of grace be done.

Behind the venerable black walnut pulpit a song leader swings his arms before introducing special singers from Chicago's wealthy but conservative Buena Memorial Presbyterian Church. The song leader of the evening, it turns out, is a student at Chicago's Northern Baptist Seminary, and gets practical work pleading for souls by taking part in about twenty meetings monthly in Chicago missions. "Sing it out!" he shouts, as he waves his arms in exaggerated gestures. The crowd echoes back,

> "O that will be glory for me,
> Glory for me, glory for me;
> When by His grace
> I shall look on His face,
> That will be glory, be glory for me."

"Sing the chorus again!" shouts the leader, and the husky voices respond. Then: "Amen! Glory for me. Glory for you, if you'll take Christ into your heart . . . tonight." Then two women singers are presented, an overflow of Buena talent and religious enthusiasm. They lose themselves "Resting in His Love":

"God has shown His loving face
From His throne in heav'n above:
And I've found a resting-place,
In the shelter of His love."

"I am resting, resting,
Resting, sweetly resting in His love;
I am resting in His love,
Resting in the shelter of His love."

"When the cares of life oppress,
When the sky is dark above;
I can always find a rest,
In the shelter of His love."
Etc.

"Time for testimonies!" sings the song leader. "Let's have a regular popcorn meeting. One right after the other. Tell what Jesus has done for you. Tell the old, old story. Are you resting in His love? You've got to admit you're a sinner. Come to Jesus for cleansing, and then you'll know His love. Amen. Who'll be first?"

On the left side of the room an old man in a gray suit jumps to his feet. "I'll be first," he says. "Everything's better since I found Jesus. Life is better. Music is better. Rivers are better. Oceans are better. Singers are better. Even the preacher sounds better."

The crowd chuckles and he sits down. There is a twitter of amens. "Who's next?" asks the leader. Nobody moves. The leader speaks: "When you don't have a cent in your pocket, God still loves you."

Another fellow, up toward the front, stands to his feet. "I'm glad God loves me," he says. Then he repeats John 3:16: "God so loved the world that He gave His only begotten Son that whosoever believeth on Him shall not perish, but have everlasting life."

There is another ripple of amens. Several other men stand to their feet. The movement is started. Testimonies come easier now. The variety is incredible; men of few years and

of many years, in every walk of life, all of them saved from
sin through the shed blood of Christ. Some of them veterans,
others babes in Christ. Some of them backsliders returned
to the fold, others as much on fire now as on their conversion
night when they staggered to the altar under the weight of
sin and were freed from its shackles.

The unbelievers look on with mixed feelings. Some are
afraid, others indifferent, some are drunk, others hungry. All
know there is something strange about this crowd of bums
that has turned to preaching. Behind the pulpit, painted on
the front wall of the mission room in letters a foot tall, is the
Scripture verse: BEHOLD THE LAMB OF GOD WHICH TAKETH AWAY
THE SIN OF THE WORLD.

The leader begs them to come to Jesus. It is seventy-five
feet from street door to pulpit; the front of the room is so
much closer than the exit, but still it is hard to go up.

It's time now for the Gospel message and the speaker reads
the twenty-third Psalm with its familiar words: "The Lord is
my shepherd, I shall not want." He gives a verse by verse
commentary, interspersed with illustrations, and then a final
appeal. Heads are bowed. "Who feels the need of prayer?
Who wants to come to Jesus? Who wants to be saved?
Raise your hand, and we'll pray for you." Some hands are
raised. Personal workers in the rear come to the help of the
prospects, and lead them forward before the prayer is finished.
Here, kneeling at the pulpit, needy souls find salvation. Personal workers quote Scripture verses, ask for an uncompro-
mised confession of guilt and sinfulness, then prod the penitents to pray. Meanwhile the leader continues the appeal:
"Come to Jesus tonight. Don't harden your heart; if God is
speaking to you, come and be saved." The pianist strikes up
softly the melody of "Just As I Am." The crowd begins to
sing:

> "Just as I am, without one plea,
> But that Thy blood was shed for me,
> And that Thou bidd'st me come to Thee,
> O Lamb of God, I come! I come!"

Suddenly Harry Saulnier appears on the platform. He's
the mission superintendent, hated and loved on State street
like few other men. Toughs have threatened to fix his wagon,
to take him for a ride, to bump him off, but Saulnier knows
they don't talk like that after finding Christ.

"Billy Sunday walked in here one night and found Christ, and then set the world afire!" he shouts. "Mel Trotter was going over to the lake to commit suicide, and he came into the mission and Jesus saved him. Gangsters, bums, hoodlums, gamblers, drunkards—they've been here, hundreds of thousands of them—and nobody was ever too bad for Jesus to save. Amen, glory! You aren't saved because you're good; if you were good, you wouldn't need to be saved. But Jesus died for your sins. He paid it all, glory to God! Make Him your Savior tonight. Come down the aisle for prayer. Come just as you are."

The piano strikes up the hymn again and the whole mission echoes electrically,

> "Just as I am, and waiting not,
> To rid my soul of one dark blot,
> To Thee whose blood can cleanse each spot,
> O Lamb of God, I come! I come!"

More people are coming down the aisles: a sailor lad from Louisiana, a college student from New York. A broken drunk can hardly manipulate his legs; a personal worker hurries to his side. Then all are taken from the mission altar to the rear office, where they kneel before a circle of chairs. Tears begin to flow; here and there a heart is breaking with grief. One man keeps saying: "I'm such a punk that Jesus can't save me." He bursts into tears. A personal worker's arms enfold him and from the Bible he reads, "Him that cometh unto Me I will in no wise cast out." He asks the man on his knees: "What does that say?" The man repeats it. "Well," says the personal worker, "have you come to Jesus?" The answer is steady: "Yes, I came tonight." "Well, will He cast you out?" The man breaks into tears again and sobs, "I hope not!" The personal worker isn't satisfied. "What do you mean—you hope not? You can be sure. Listen . . ." Then he reads again the Scripture verse, and goes through the whole conversation. This time the man becomes a man of faith. "I know He's my Savior," he says and jumps to his feet. Over in the corner of the mission office someone takes his name and address and records another spiritual birthday.

The convert looks around the room and sees a half-dozen others praying through. "It's like being a new man," he says. Then one of the workers shows him to supper and to a

night's lodging.   By morning the office will have several leads
for a job at which this salvaged soul can work and walk into
a new life.

Out in the mission hall everything is now quiet.  The place
is deserted; the men are down at supper and on their way to
bed.  But there is a strange halo around the empty old chairs
'u which men like Harry Monroe, Billy Sunday, Mel Trotter
Dick Lane, John Calahan, Robert Atkinson, Rob "Razor"
Fenton, Tom Mackey, Dick Ramey, and scores of others sat
and grappled with Satan, until, in the strength of God's grace,
they tore themselves loose from those old chairs—valued by
fire insurance underwriters today at forty cents apiece—and
walked the trail to salvation in Christ.

## CHAPTER III

## THE ANGEL OF THE SLUMS

The catastrophic fire of 1871 scattered Chicago churches to the city's outskirts, but kindled in its wake a flare of saloons, brothels and gambling halls. Rather than to abandon the Loop to this iniquity and vice, Colonel and Mrs. George R. Clarke wedged the first rescue mission of its kind in the Northwest into Whiskey Row, at 386 South Clark street. September 15, 1877, was its inaugural day.

No seminary training, no prophetic gift was theirs, but an unquenchable passion for souls charged their lives. "Saloons were on either side of us, noise and confusion almost baffled us," she wrote, "but Mr. Clarke preached and I tried my best to keep crooked men straight."

The former Sarah Dunn, born November 13, 1835, in New York's Cayuga county, Mrs. Clarke attended Sunday school just like many another person and was safeguarded by Christian parents from cards, theaters and dances. She longed often to become a Christian, but nobody spoke to her personally about her soul until 1855. Returning from a visit at Wilkesbarre Seminary, she was asked by an acquaintance waiting with her on the Scranton Depot platform to "give your heart to God." The promise was made. Mrs. Clarke dated her conversion from that moment when cathedral joy flooded her soul.

After teaching school in Elmira, New York, she moved in 1861 to Waterloo, Iowa. It was there that a redirecting revelation changed her life ambitions. Faithful in church relations, she was nevertheless a stranger to real consecration. One day while completing an elaborate decoration for the family home she seemed to hear an audible voice, as if from heaven, "What are you doing to decorate your heavenly home?"

Haunted by this question, Sarah resolved to forget perishable earthly adornments and to seek to "adorn the heavenly mansion through all the cycles of eternity." The salvation of sinners grew into an absorbing, consuming passion. Moving to Chicago a few years later, she compromised conscience and time sufficiently by making fashionable calls to assure her social standing. Then, quite penitently, garbed in less costly clothes, she carried on a visitation program among the poor. Such delight became hers in supplying the needs of these unfortunates and in leading them to Christ that she "was at once convinced my mission in life had been revealed."

With a growing number of poor families on her list, she rallied a few friends in 1869 into starting a mission Sunday school at State and Twenty-Third streets. During those years, in a business transaction, she met Colonel George R. Clarke, prominent realtor and Civil War veteran. They were married in 1873, two years after the great Chicago fire, and after four merry years in the fashionable circle to which Colonel Clarke clung despite his Christianity, they decided to abandon their up-and-outer friends to their Cyrenaic philosophy and to lead their down-and-outer prospects to Christ. Colonel Clarke had a reputation as "the poorest preacher that ever tried to expound God's Word," but as Mrs. Clarke prayed, and her husband preached, the Gospel spread through the slums, and sinners found the trail to heaven.

Mr. Clarke, too, was a native of New York state, born February 22, 1827, in Otsego county, only to travel westward for study at Beloit College, Beloit, Wisconsin. After graduation he became principal of Milton Academy, edited a paper called the Sauk County Standard, and studied law. Although admitted to the bar in 1853, he turned his attention to real estate. The new business carried him to Colorado for two years and there, among the miners, only a divine overpowering kept him from shady land deals. God used his sainted mother's prayers to awaken his conscience, and after great agony of repentance for sin came the assurance of Christ's atonement.

When the Civil War broke out in 1860, Clarke returned to Chicago and secured recruits for the 113th Illinois Volunteers. Made captain of that company, then later promoted to major and lieutenant colonel, he served with distinction. At the close of the war, back in Chicago, Colonel Clarke resumed real estate activities and formed the acquaintance of Sarah Dunn, who already had started her peculiar Sunday school venture for the poor. The little mission Sunday school enlisted his growing interest, too, and soon Colonel Clarke was concerned over the example and influence of his Christian testimony, heretofore quite without distinction. More and more funds customarily devoted to Cuban cigars and the entertainment of guests were diverted to Christian effort.

Mrs. Clarke's conscience was troubling her also. Convicted of a misuse of God's time in social functions, she persuaded Colonel Clarke to visit the slums along the levee—the stretch of South Clark street from Van Buren to Twenty-Second street—with its overflow of drunkards and outcasts, male and female. Gambling halls, saloons and brothels had infested the districts. The Colonel was interested in a humanitarian sense, but he had no intention of founding a mission. He had other plans, especially an ambition to acquire great wealth.

For a time it seemed Mrs. Clarke's vision of a united ministry among the needy was hopeless, but she never abandoned it as a secret subject of prayer. A business scheme with great remunerative prospects that carried Colonel Clarke to the Rocky Mountains threatened to fell the final possibility of a rescue mission. Mrs. Clarke agonized many hours in prayer. It was no surprise then that while the Colonel laid his plans for riches, the Spirit of God spoke to him with sharp conviction. Alone with God a thousand miles from home, he fell to his knees and consecrated himself to divine service for mission work. He telegraphed his wife of his change of life purposes and added that he was returning to Chicago at once to join her in founding a mission.

On September 15, 1877, at 386 South Clark street, Chicago, the first rescue mission in the Northwest flung open its doors. Only five years earlier the world's first rescue mission had been founded by Jerry McAuley on October 8, 1872, at 316 Water Street, New York. Word spread from both places that the drunkard was more welcome than the tee-totaler, the thief than the policeman, the harlot than the choir singer. How aware Mother Clarke was of the New York enterprise, if at all, is unknown.

The Clarkes proudly opened house in the tiny store. Fitted with long, wooden, backless benches, the mission boasted a seating capacity of forty. Oil lamps flickered from the side walls. The stove was of ancient design, but it gave heat. The old organ groaned, but it was better than none. The rest of the paraphernalia was limited to a few huge signs painted on the walls. One of them, centered halfway across the front, read GOD IS LOVE. That on the left wall read THOU GOD SEEST ME.

On the right was the great invitation COME UNTO ME ALL YE THAT LABOR AND ARE HEAVY LADEN AND I WILL GIVE YOU REST. There was no pulpit, only a chair and table used by Colonel Clarke.

The Colonel was no evangelist nor pulpit orator. Friends hesitated even to rate him among the world's worst preachers. But God was there in approval of a ministry steeped in tender compassion for the souls of men. As he talked to boisterous crowds, often on John 3:16, his favorite text, tears ran from Colonel Clarke's cheeks. He was regarded by some as the most easily affected man ever born.

The influx of men was under way. Without order and without respect they came, many of them drunk beyond consciousness. It was no small job just to maintain a minimum of boisterousness. Mrs. Clarke seemed to possess a remarkable influence over the offenders, a service which she accomplished usefully throughout all her years of mission work. But even amid the confused babbling of drunkards, God's presence was manifested. During the very first days four persons professed conversion, three giving evidence of a real conversion experience. The Clarkes had put out the fleece. Night after night the old, old story of Jesus and His power to save rang out to patrons of brothels, gambling joints and opium dens. Night after night thieves, harlots and alcoholics were loosed from Satan's chains and wooed through the Clarkes' ministry into the loving heart of God. The nets of God were straining with precious souls.

CHAPTER IV

## THE SHIFT TO PACIFIC BEER GARDEN

"Colonel Clarke's Mission," as it was called, continued on
the south Clark street levee only for three or four years, for a
golden opportunity came as if overnight.

The lease of the Pacific Beer Garden, regarded as the most
notorious, murderous joint west of New York City, was for
sale. Located on Van Buren street, between Clark and Dear-
born, the site was better than the Clark street location in
many respects. Here where the vilest and toughest groups
gathered for cheap beer, just around the corner from dens of
ribald and licentious women, was the very district in which to
plant the growing mission. Recalling a few real estate prin-
ciples, the Colonel interviewed the owners and struck a deal.

Shortly thereafter, during one of Dwight L. Moody's visits
to Chicago, Colonel Clarke mentioned the transfer to the
Pacific Beer Garden and asked the great evangelist to suggest
an opportune name for the refuge. Moody, then on an evangelistic circuit of American cities after having stirred England
as only Wesley and Whitefield had done previously, replied
at once: "Strike out the 'beer' and add the word 'mission.'"
And so it became "Pacific Garden Mission." No stranger to the
work of the Clarkes, Moody called the mission "the greatest on
earth," and not infrequently fished there for men himself.

Down-and-outers struck a new trail to 100 East Van Buren
street, where, from 1880 onward, the Pacific Garden Mission
occupied a good-sized room on the corner of Fourth avenue
and Van Buren street. In 1909 Chicago changed its street
numbering system, and the address became 67 West Van
Buren street. Fourth avenue became Custom House Place,
and still later, Federal street. But the rescue house through
the years maintained a ring-side seat on sinners' lane, and
used the larger quarters to good advantage. Needy men found
their way into the gloomy interior, dimly lighted by kerosene
lamps, heated by barrel stoves. There was always a heartfelt
welcome by "Mother" Clarke who showed them a seat on the
hard wooden benches, and who turned their tossed spirits to
the sure Word of God.

Nobody, however rowdy, was ever turned away from the meetings until "Mother" Clarke gave the word. When the service began, order was imperative. If a man became noisy, an usher would politely ask him to become quiet for the sake of the others who wanted to hear the singing and speaking. If the request was not heeded, "Mother" Clarke herself would walk back, place her arm tenderly around the drunkard and whisper, "You must be still now, for we want to tell you about Jesus, your Savior." Then she returned to the platform. If the noise persisted, a slight signal from "Mother" Clarke which the ushers recognized, authorized some of the half-dozen saintly "bouncers" to lift the offender bodily into the air, out the door, and to stand him firmly on his feet again. From the beginning it was a rule of the mission that no drunkard should ever be permitted to disturb a meeting.

One night, accordingly, a drunkard too delirious for reasoning was ushered from the room. Unknown to him a New Testament had been slipped inside his coat pocket alongside the troublesome whiskey flask. When the next morning he found the flask broken, he nevertheless realized his pocket was not empty. With amazement he opened the New Testament. On the fly-leaf was written, "From one who is praying for you." Thus reminded of his saintly mother who for years had placed him first on her prayer list, the drunkard battled conviction for some days and then returned to the mission to acknowledge Christ as Savior.

On another night a curious drunk, not daring to venture inside, yet wanting to know what took place, climbed up the gas pole in front of the mission and looked through the open transom. On the front wall his eyes met the words which were not visible through the frost-covered windows: "The Son of Man came to seek and to save them that are lost." It was the beginning of a heart restlessness that was not stilled until, at a return visit to the mission, this time inside, Christ became his Savior.

Men and women of all ages, levels and color sat in that dingy room and forgot the darkness as Colonel Clarke preached the light of Jesus as the Savior of the world. They came from barrel-houses, as the low drinking places were then called, from far and near. Under the mission itself was what appeared to be a basement laundry, but which was actually an opium dive. The adjacent shoe shop was a blind for a gambling house. Stretching south from Van Buren was the red light district, and in every direction were cheap saloons. The tinny banjos and other instruments wailing from bar-rooms were heard on every street, but soon the old mission organ sent its triumphant melody to the heart of this vicious district of defeated mankind.

"Hope For All Who Enter" read the sign over the mission doorway, and it was true. Derelicts, women of the streets, the flotsam and jetsam of a great city, came nightly to hear Colonel and Mrs. Clarke tell the story of Jesus and His power to save. One by one, brands were snatched from the burning, and they went out to win others for Christ. Accordingly the mission was becoming more loved and more hated. In addition to its regular ministry, prison and hospital visitation was fostered, and in that mission Chicago's first free kindergarten was begun.

Twice a week Mrs. Clarke spent afternoons visiting from cell to cell in the county jail. Among the many jail converts was a John Callahan. Arrested in New York and sent to a reformatory, Callahan had made his escape, and drifted to Chicago where he joined a notorious west side gang. The law finally captured him, and now, awaiting trial, he was visited in his cell by Mrs. Clarke. Butch Lyon, Callahan's cell-mate, jumped on the top bunk with derisive laughter, not wanting the "angel of mercy" to deal with him. Callahan, on the other hand, fell to the floor and prayed for mercy. After serving a term in Joliet, Callahan went to Minneapolis, where, instead of tending bar as he had once done, he walked into a mission and into newness of life in Christ Jesus. Butch Lyon met death on the gallows. John Callahan was born again and became superintendent of the Hadley Rescue Hall on New York City's Bowery.

On another afternoon, so hot and sultry that workers were tempted to omit the jail visitation, but finally decided that human need rather than the weather should dictate to their spirits, a forlorn, broken-hearted man in desperate need of God sat in cell 79. He fell to his knees, pleaded for forgiveness and then arose, a new creature. Turning for his tobacco, he suddenly shrank from it, declaring: "No! I must never touch that weed again." For twenty-four years he proclaimed the grace of God in Christian service as a faithful mission worker.

During those years the cost of the mission was borne by the personal income of the Clarkes. With the shift to Van Buren street, expenses for rent and general maintenance were quite heavy, especially since the Colonel's income had been somewhat limited now with his full-time application to mission effort.

The day came when there was not enough money in view to pay the rent. It was necessary to meet the obligation promptly. Colonel and Mrs. Clarke prayed all night long for the Lord to send them rent money, so the bill could be met on time the following night. Demands for mission lodgings had increased, and the reclamation of sinners showed constant advance. They could not tolerate the idea of shutting the mission for a single night. Though never discouraged, the question why God should permit them to come to such financial stringency when the work was being carried forward so faithfully crept into their hearts. Finally they determined not to question divine wisdom, but merely to pray and trust.

The next morning God sent manna from heaven in nineteenth century terms. The entire front yard of the Clarkes' Morgan Park home was covered with mushrooms of the best quality. The event was the more mysterious because the plants appeared in advance of the regular season. With thanksgiving the mushrooms were gathered and sold to the then already famous Palmer House. There was enough and to spare. The rent was paid and also other mission expenses met. In her booklet, "God Is Love," written thirty-five years later by "Mother" Clarke, she commented: "No mushrooms were ever seen there before—nor any since."

Though the Clarkes' private income previously had not been meager, the thought impressed them both that valuable indulgences of their early society years might well be disposed of to carry on the Lord's work. Diamonds and jewelry of every description, valued presents, and other items were converted into cash for the conversion of sinners. It was a tremendous step of faith, but God blessed it, for in its wake came an opportunity for Clarke to invest in a mining operation by which he realized sufficient income to adjust his business matters and to run the mission for ten years.

"Mother" Clarke herself sometimes became almost niggardly as to her own comfort, in order to save money for the mission. At mission board meetings, whenever the treasurer found a deficit he merely handed the statement to "Mother" Clarke, who immediately wrote a personal check for the shortage. She ate the most common lunches and walked unbelievable distances to save small change. Nor would she be shaken from the habit.

During the mission's early days, railroad accommodations were poor. Only a dummy train, morning and evening, with a midnight train on the same line, ran anywhere near the Clarke home. A considerable walk always remained at that. One night, when the Clarkes took the midnight train as usual after a strenuous day, they were obliged to make the two-mile walk from the station to their residence through a terrific storm, facing heavy rain and sleet all the way. When entering the house, Mrs. Clarke later related, she "found his satanic majesty on hand, and with a modest voice he inquired, 'Does it pay?' I emphatically replied, 'Yes. I'd walk ten miles— or all night—if I could be the means of winning a soul.'" After that, she said, the devil never accosted her again along those lines.

Day after day the Clarkes continued. With methodical precision, "Mother" Clarke entered the mission door, went to Room Twelve for prayer, proceeded to the mission workers' prayer meeting, and then took her place on the platform. Colonel Clarke would turn the pages of his Bible, join the personal workers for prayer, and then start the meeting. Together they worked in the joy of bringing many souls to Christ. They were an incomparable team of consecrated workers for God. It was a great task for Christ and His kingdom, and as the Clarkes carried it forward, they fell more and more deeply in love. On his sixty-third birthday, in 1890, Colonel Clarke wrote:

### ODE TO MY BELOVED WIFE ON MY SIXTY-THIRD BIRTHDAY

I'm sixty-three today, dear wife,
  How quickly time has sped,
The larger part of childhood's friends,
  Lie mouldering with the dead;
But since our paths of life were joined,
  A happy life I've led.

I've marched along with you, dear wife,
　Our steps with knee to knee,
My heart enrapted with you, my dear,
　And your warm heart with me;
For thus, dear wife, it ever should,
　With married people be.

A truer wife than you have been,
　Since we were joined IN ONE,
Ne'er sat beneath the moon's pale light,
　Or walked beneath the sun;
I well might say till then, dear wife,
　My life had not begun.

'Tis true it has not been, dear wife,
　All "rose without a thorn,"
How could it be, since we were wed,
　On such a stormy morn;
And yet the many cares of life,
　Have all been sweetly borne.

No child has graced our wedded life,
　In all these passing years,
Nor have we nights of vigil kept,
　O'er such with anxious fears;
Nor death has filled for us a cup,
　With sorrow and with tears.

Not oft we've sat around our hearth,
　On winter's stormy night,
To look upon the glowing coals,
　Of fires burning bright,
But trust we've brought to darken'd hearts,
　A little more of light.

The pleasure-seeking world, my dear,
　To us has been unknown,
As year by year away from it,
　We steadily have grown;
And yet, dear wife, apart from it,
　We ne'er have lived alone.

In living thus for others, dear,
　We've found a solace sweet,
As we have tried to lessen some
　The tramp of weary feet;
And caused some aching hearts, I trust,
　More cheerfully to beat.

We have not traveled far from home,
　While traveling every day,
Nor have we seen the wondrous sights,
　Of countries far away;
But we have homeward led again
　*Some feet* which went astray.

We've worshiped not in churches grand,
  Or sat in cushioned pews,
But we have told to sinful men,
  The Gospel! *Blessed news;*
And filled with holy oil I trust,
  Some widow's empty cruse.

Not much have we to leave the world,
  Of silver and of gold,
Nor large estate, nor titled names,
  Of lineage grand and old;
Nor have we lived a selfish life,
  With hardened hearts and cold.

But then, dear wife, I trust we leave,
  A little brighter place,
In some once darkened hearts on earth,
  (Before they saw our face),
Which more than *wealth* or *fame,* my dear.
  May benefit our race.

The blessed Lord who loves us, dear,
  Has very faithful been,
To knit our hearts together, love,
  And keep our pathway green;
And all along His guiding hand,
  In everything is seen.

There's no such thing as growing old,
  To loving hearts and true,
Each year has brought a sweeter joy,
  To me, my dear, and you;
To us the oft recurring years,
  Bring always something new.

We've climbed the hill together, dear,
  And passed the summit o'er,
Not far ahead we see the light,
  Of Beulah's happy shore;
Soon we shall see the face of Him,
  Our hearts so much adore.

And when the night of death comes on,
  Perhaps "the white winged dove,"
May bear our souls together, dear,
  To live with Christ above;
And share together with His saints,
  The treasures of His love.

And He may grant us then to see,
  The good that we have done,
The many happy souls that we,
  To Him perhaps have won,
As at his pierced feet we lay
  The golden sheaves all down.

> So let us plod along, dear wife,
>   As we are wont to go,
> And scatter seeds of kindness, dear,
>   On saddened hearts below,
> And trust the *Lord* to gather in
>   The harvest that we sow.

Two and one-half years later, on June 22, 1892, the Colonel was dead. During the fifteen years they had worked side by side, the mission had never closed its doors a night. Nor would God be afar off now: His man for the gap was already chosen.

## CHAPTER V

## FROM COUNTERFEITING TO REALITY

When a Detroit federal judge singled out and freed an Irish lad from a gang of counterfeiters on trial in federal court, he gave Harry Monroe a first shove toward heaven.

"You don't belong with that crowd," said the judge.

Harry never felt less like belonging with them than at that moment. Bad from head to foot and hard-boiled to the core, he nevertheless couldn't keep back the tears. Those were the first really kind words he had heard since leaving home.

"Your honor, I believe if I had half a chance I would go straight, I'm so tired of it all."

The judge stood up and put his hand on Harry's shoulder. The lad wasn't charged with making counterfeit money; some of the others did that. He merely "shoved the queer," as they called passing the fake bills along to innocent victims.

Harry wept and waited for the judge to speak. "I trust God and I trust you," said the man, "to carry on."

Harry bounded for the first train to Chicago. He had little money, but from the Windy City depot he went that night to the first big saloon within sight and ordered a schooner of beer. The saloon clock showed 7:30 when he lifted the glass to his lips. Suddenly he stopped.

"If I drink that," he thought, "I'm right back where I was."

An electric tingle surged through him. Replacing the glass on the bar, Harry Monroe walked out. As he turned the corner, a door opened on Van Buren street, pushing music and singing in its sweep. Monroe stopped, then walked inside.

It was a Saturday night in February, 1880, in Pacific Garden Mission. When Colonel Clarke came down at the close of the meeting and asked Monroe to give his heart to Jesus, the lad answered: "You stick to your business and I'll stick to mine." It was a queer response from one destined for 35 years after that to be a close friend of the rescue mission, for 20 years its superintendent.

Harry Monroe came from Exeter, New Hampshire, where he was born January 17, 1853. His fondness for drink soon introduced him to the wrong crowd. In Chicago he was no stranger to Whiskey Row, where he lost what money he had in the gambling dens, and where he saw many of his friends go to drunkards' graves. Before long he was associated with an outfit that made and passed counterfeit money. Caught in a police net, he was only 27 when he appeared for a hearing in Detroit before the federal judge who told him to go straight.

The night Monroe surprised himself by wandering into Pacific Garden Mission, after an aimless shamble along the street, he heard some of the very men who had formerly quaffed the cup on Whiskey Row. They told of Christ's power to change lives and their words rang true. Speaker of that particular evening was D. W. Potter, prominent Chicago banker, who took charge of the meetings one night a week.

Monroe shook from top to bottom, but concealed his reaction effectively and sufficiently to rebuff Colonel Clarke's invitation to become a Christian.

The big-hearted colonel understood. Smothering Monroe's trembling hand in his own, he said: "Young man, do you know that Jesus loves you and so do I?" Then the colonel told of his wonderful Savior, of Christ's power to save others, and of His promise to cover all the past with His shed blood, and to give men a new start.

"A new start?" questioned Monroe. "How?"

Colonel Clarke told him and Monroe was converted that very night. "I quit booze from this minute on," he said, and then bowed his head for prayer. "God be merciful to me, a sinner," he blurted, as the colonel led him along toward the front of the mission, "and save me for Jesus' sake."

Harry Monroe told that story over and over. "I've never regretted that prayer for a moment," he'd say, outlining the life from which Jesus saved him. As he told of his past life of gambling and drink to the listening derelicts gathered in the mission, he had a habit of closing his eyes, as though the experiences of the days and nights he was recounting were too painfully vivid.

The night Harry was converted he was lodged by the colonel in a cheap room. Before retiring he wrote his Massachusetts mother for the first time in twelve years. She thought he was dead.

Harry didn't sleep a wink all night. The hours were too filled with praise to God for the new chance to make good in life. Looking back over the years he saw nothing but dismal failure; looking into the future, he saw only glory.

The next day was Sunday. At the mission Harry Monroe gave his first testimony, sending a thrill of joy through the crowd. It was only a few weeks until Colonel and Mrs. Clarke had him helping in the meetings. Learning of his ability to sing, they gave him charge of the song service. Hymns and Gospel songs throbbed with new life as Harry pulled more singing out of that nondescript bunch of tramps in the old mission refuge than many a preacher ever evinced from the best robed choir. He was determined to pour the Gospel music all the way down Whiskey Row, where he himself had lost a small fortune, buying tickets to hell.

Harry was a barber shop tenor. Night after night he would sing, "Tell Mother I'll Be There," and then relate how he found Christ in the mission and wrote the same night to the mother who thought him dead. "Steady, now," he would say; "let's bow our heads while I sing the chorus once again." Then his voice would fill the hall:

> "Tell mother I'll be there
> In answer to her prayer;
> This message, blessed Savior, to her bear!
> Tell mother I'll be there,
> Heav'n's joys with her to share;
> Yes, tell my darling mother I'll be there!"

Then he would pray and give the invitation. Hands would go up for prayer before the message of the evening had been given.

Perhaps as he turned in reflection upon his own redeemed life, Harry Monroe's vision of the fields white unto harvest grew into an unending horizon upon which he looked with penetrating compassion. Porky and of medium height rather than pudgy, he had a fondness for blue serge suits. Kindliness glowed from his face, so frank and unadorned in its general squareness, yet so adamant in its structural strength. He had a ready wit which flowed from his lips. The grimness of those lips, once the mouthpiece for the issues of everlasting death, now heralded the glad tidings of eternal life. The bushy eyebrows once knit in a formidable plotting of crime now cupped the gleam of unravelling twisted lives. The hair on his head was vanishing and there were furrows on his face. What must once have been the marks of sin, God's grace had softened into lines of sympathy and understanding. This Harry Monroe, heavy and squared in general impress with modifying strokes of graduated boldness throughout his face, could unashamedly raise his high voice in testimony to Him who maketh all things new.

From the very start he was a soul-winner. His passion to win the lost kept him pleading and praying until victory and newness of life came to seeking hearts. Nor would Harry Monroe stop there. He shepherded his spiritual children as his very own, seeking out respectable jobs and helpful environments and feeding them more and more with the Bread of Life.

It was not unusual then, that when Colonel Clarke died in 1892, Harry Monroe should succeed his spiritual father as superintendent of Pacific Garden Mission. Together with Mrs. Clarke he held high the Savior of men to mission crowds until 1912, when he answered briefly the call to nation-wide evangelistic service.

## Chapter VI

## LOADING THE BASES ON THE SAWDUST TRAIL

Billy Sunday never saw his father who walked thirty miles to enlist in the Civil War and died with scores of other Iowa infantrymen after fording a partly frozen river. From the front lines he had written the expectant mother, "If it is a boy, name him William Ashley." Mother and children lived in the Ames, Iowa, log cabin for years before they managed to move into a frame house. Perhaps that accounted for Billy Sunday's illness the first three years of his life, which an itinerant doctor cured with a syrup stewed from wild roots.

The lad had an intense love for his grandmother. When she died, the family did not tell Billy for two days. Heartbroken, he mourned at the casket, refusing to be moved. The second day after the funeral Billy vanished; no searching party could locate him. Finally his pet dog picked the scent through the snow, and, leading the posse to the cemetery, stopped where the lad lay thrown across the grave, chill-bitten by a cold November wind, and sobbing so that the friends despaired of his ever stopping. For weeks his life was at low ebb, but the healing tide finally came.

The wolf of poverty hovered constantly at the log cabin door, so that Sunday's mother finally decided to put her two boys in a nearby soldiers' orphanage. She prayed and wept while the boys slept on the train. When Billy said "goodbye" he never dreamed that for the last thirty years of his mother's life, which ended June 25, 1918, he would have the joy of providing a really decent home for her. That last June morning when he called her to breakfast she had gone on to heaven without stopping to kiss her boy "goodbye."

Sunday's first job after leaving the orphanage in his midteens was mopping a hotel which he also served as barker, orating its advantages to incoming train arrivals. Three months of that was enough. Then, learning that Iowa's lieutenant governor needed a boy, he polished his shoes, had his hair trimmed, and convinced Colonel John Scott's wife that he, Billy Sunday, was the young man qualified for the job.

Colonel and Mrs. Scott sent him to high school, where, after
two years he became school janitor, meanwhile continuing
his odd jobs for the lieutenant governor.

His baseball career began with a local team in Marshalltown, Iowa, for which Sunday played left field. It so happened that Pop Anson, captain of Chicago's famous National
league White Sox (now the Cubs), spent his winters in
Marshalltown. When the topic turned to baseball, which
was Anson's usual diet, he found the townspeople talking
about Billy Sunday's speed on the diamond and his ability to
nab fly balls that nobody else would even attempt catching.
Considering that Sunday could run three hundred yards in
thirty-four seconds, it was no surprise that he caught flies like
some folks catch a cold. Cap Anson's aunt, who lived in
Marshalltown, urged the sportsman to take Billy to Chicago
for a trial. In the spring, accordingly, a telegram summoned
young Sunday for a Windy City tryout. Buying a new green
suit for six dollars and borrowing money for the trip, Billy
met the captain.

On Sunday's first day on the diamond, Anson set the lad to
a foot race against Fred Pfeffer, crack runner for the Chicago
team. Sunday had no running shoes, so ran barefoot. He
not only won the race by fifteen feet, but won his way into
the hearts of the players. Cap Anson tossed him a twenty-
dollar gold piece.

During his first few seasons, Sunday succeeded in batting
so poorly that the team considered it a total mistake when he
actually did connect. He struck out the first thirteen times at
the plate. Thereafter he began to find his stride.

Sunday broke into professional baseball when its players
were rough, profane and hard-drinking fighters. He did not
need much encouragement for profanity himself, nor was he
adverse to wine and beer. During the winter months he attended Northwestern University; during the summer he
whacked the horsehide. He proved a splendid base-runner
and a brilliant fielder. Seldom faring exceptionally in the
batter's box against professional pitchers, he nevertheless in
one game got a home run and a single against an outstanding
twirler. He was at his best when he stole four bases while
Connie Mack of the Philadelphia Athletics was catching.

Sunday's later pulpit pre-eminence did not spin a halo about
his previous athletic success; rather his evangelistic success

gained added glow from the days on the diamond, for he was known to sports fans of his generation as the speediest base-runner and most daring base-stealer in baseball. In his earlier days he took too many chances, and his judgment was not always sound. But his control over the ball enabled him to throw straight and swiftly, and he was so fast on his feet that more than one top-rate player threw wild in the effort to head him off. He could stretch ordinary one-base hits into doubles without trouble to anyone but the opposing team, and he was the first man to run the circuit of bases in fourteen seconds.

In 1886, when Sunday had been three years on the Chicago nine, he walked down State street one Sunday afternoon with some of the biggest names in baseball. (In those days they played no Sunday games, for there would have been no crowds.) The party entered a saloon, had a round of drinks, then walked to the vacant lot at State and Van Buren streets. Whenever Billy Sunday passed that lot in later years, even when Siegel & Cooper's big department store had been erected over it, he took off his hat, bowed his head and thanked God for saving him. Forty years after Sunday's decision, a policeman saw him stop and close his eyes in the midst of a crowd. He offered to call a wagon if the man felt sick. Billy Sunday introduced himself and held a one-man street meeting.

When Sunday and his baseball associates reached State and Van Buren on that memorable day, some men and women in a horse-drawn wagon were playing horns, flutes and slide trombones, and were singing hymns he had heard in Sunday school and which his mother used to sing in the Iowa log cabin. The baseball crowd sat on the curbstone and listened. Suddenly a winsome, square-faced Irishman arose. That was Harry Monroe. He told how he once passed counterfeit money for a gang of criminals and how he had been converted at Pacific Garden Mission.

"Don't you men want to hear the story," said Monroe, as he stepped toward the curb, "of other men who used to be dips, yeggs, burglars, second-story workers, and who today are respectable and have fine families? Or women who were slaves to dope and drink, or harlots who sold their womanhood in the red light districts here, and who are now married in happy homes? Come down to the mission tonight at 100 East Van Buren and you'll hear stories that will stir you, even if you've never been inside a church, or if you've wandered far away from God and your mother's religion."

Billy Sunday turned to the fellows at his side and said, "Boys, I'm saying goodbye to the old life." Some of the men chuckled, others laughed, others were serious. Some of them paid no attention at all.

That night at the mission Sunday was fascinated by the testimonies of men who went from the guttermost to the uppermost. Again and again he attended and one night he went forward and publicly professed Christ as Savior.

The night he went forward he was not drunk, despite the story to that effect. Unfortunately, Sunday himself gave that story credence when, in relating his conversion experience, he declared that he "knocked over several chairs getting to the front." Harry Monroe had given the message and Sunday was under tremendous conviction. Mother Clarke came back to his side and said, putting her arm around Billy, "Young man, God loves you. Jesus died for you, and He wants you to love Him and give your heart to Him." The ball player could no longer resist. He swung clumsily around the chairs, walked to the front and sat down. Harry Monroe came to his side and they knelt for prayer.

The next three nights Billy Sunday never slept a wink. He dreaded the jibes of the ball team at ten o'clock Wednesday morning practice and during the afternoon game. He trembled when he walked out to the field. There was Mike Kelly, one of Chicago's outstanding stars, coming toward him. Mike was a Catholic, and Billy expected almost anything. "Billy," he said, "I've read in the papers what you've done. Religion isn't my long suit. It's a long time since I've been to mass. But I won't knock you, and if anyone does, I'll knock him." Then came the rest of the team, all of them, to pat Billy on the back and wish him the best of luck. They were at a loss for words, too, and Sunday felt as if a millstone had dropped from his neck.

Billy Sunday became even a better baseball player. He always insisted that taking Christ as Savior will make a man better at whatever he does, providing it's a decent job. That afternoon the Chicago team was pitted against Detroit, one of the hardest hitting squads in the country. The Detroiters could be behind nine to nothing at the start of the ninth, and yet push over ten runs in the final inning; they had a reputation for redeeming themselves. This day, Chicago eked out a narrow lead right to the last inning. The Chicago twirler, John Clarkson, one of the greatest pitchers of the day, had worked his famous "zipper" ball, with an illusory upshoot, overtime. Two Detroit batters went down in the ninth. Billy Sunday, playing right field, called in, "One more, John, and they're done!" The next batter was Charlie Bennett, Detroit catcher, who hit right-handed and nine times out of ten sailed the horsehide deep into right center field. Sunday was playing far back, and followed five speedy tosses, while Bennett came through with two strikes and three balls. The Chicagoans knew that Bennett couldn't hit a high ball close to the body, but he could set a low ball off like dynamite. Clarkson braced himself for a bullet-ball high and inside. His foot slipped. The ball went low. The resultant crack of ball and bat echoed through the stands.

Over in right field Billy Sunday saw it whirling through the sky, far over his head. Like a bolt of lightning he turned. Following the approximate course, he ran so fast he forgot he could do one hundred yards in ten seconds flat. As he ran, he prayed, "Lord, I'm on the spot, and now I'm a Christian. If you ever help me, please do it now."

The grandstand and bleachers were wild with excitement and thunderous shouting. To the crowd standing along the right field wall Sunday yelled, "Get out of the way!" Through the opening he sped, stopped, stuck his hand into the clouds with a leap. His fingers closed over the ball. As he landed, he lost balance and fell, but jumped up with the horsehide secure in his hand.

The crowd went almost insane. Pop bottles, hats, cushions, and practically everything else went flying into the air. Tom Johnson, later mayor of Cleveland, threw his arms around Billy and shoved a ten dollar bill into his hand. At the clubhouse the whole team gave him a cheer, took off his uniform and dressed him up. Then the crowd rushed in, carrying him off on its shoulders. At the gate, brown-eyed, black-haired Helen Thompson threw her arms around him and kissed him. She was the Mrs. Sunday-to-be.

Not many days later when the Chicago team traveled to a St. Louis series, Sunday happened into a second-hand book store and for thirty-five cents bought his first Bible. At the end of the season he joined the Bible class of Chicago's Central Y. M. C. A., back in the days—as Mrs. Sunday still puts it—"when the Y had Bibles, not billiards."

After Sunday's conversion in 1886, he spent three additional years with the Chicago team. The people in the stands as well as his teammates knew that he had a working religion. On Sundays he gave Y. M. C. A. talks, for which he was in great demand, and the sports pages all alluded to his church activity. An apt Bible student, he often testified, gave a brief Bible message, and then an invitation. He developed increasing ability as a personal worker. Whenever the team traveled around the country, Sunday was booked for meetings in local churches or with Bible clubs eager to hear his testimony.

When he left the Chicago team, it was to spend a year each with the Pittsburgh and Philadelphia clubs, but it was not difficult to discern that his interest in full-time Christian service was growing. Five years after his conversion, Sunday obtained a release from the three-year contract with Philadelphia in order to enter some form of Christian service. No sooner done than Jim Hart of the Cincinnati team pushed a $3,500 contract under his eyes. It was a tremendous temptation, especially when Billy's baseball friends told him it was the opportunity of a lifetime. After all, players are on the diamond only seven months of the year, and Hart was including the first month's $500 check in advance. That night Sunday prayed, not stopping until five o'clock the next morning. He refused Hart's offer.

Billy's alternative, that of going into Y. M. C. A. work as a subordinate secretary at $83.33 per month, which sometimes proved as much as six months' overdue, seemed a great anticlimax to his baseball friends. To Sunday, that decisive March of 1891 was one of the greatest parting of the ways in his life.

## CHAPTER VII

## MEL TROTTER'S SUICIDE NIGHT

Born May 15, 1870, at Orangeville, Illinois, Mel Trotter was five years of age when the family moved to nearby Polo. His start in life was hardly auspicious. Mel had little schooling. His father wanted him to continue, but it was the son himself who considered an education unnecessary for success. What's more, the father was a drunkard, and the three sons after him. Often the boys tended bar for their own father.

When Mel was seventeen, the family removed to Freeport, Illinois, where Mel turned independent and learned barbering. Soon he was drawing a man's salary.

"That's a bad thing for a boy," he said later. "I was able to indulge in many things that did me harm."

Two years later he went to Pearl City, Iowa, to work his trade. There he fell into drinking and gambling, lost his job, and went to Davenport, Iowa, to do insurance work.

"I got to know a great deal about four-legged trotters," Mel used to say. "I was always stuck on the finest horses and I was a good fellow. I kept on drinking and the first thing I knew, I couldn't stop. The friends I had, found that when they needed me most I wasn't there to help, so they cut me out, and finally I got to drinking sheenies, three for five.

"And I couldn't help it. I tried to break away and get into the country. A fellow named Cook gave me a dandy black horse, one of the best I ever drove, and so I got a buggy and a job in the country where I made a lot of money. My wife went with me to keep me sober. I would stay sober a little while, and I really wanted to. I'd say, 'I'll never take another drink as long as I live.'"

One night, after a long drive, Mel went to put the horse in the barn. His wife went to the house. It was snowing, and a bitter-cold Iowa day. Suddenly the devil seemed to get hold of him. Although Mel had driven the horse nearly as fast and hard as he would go, he nevertheless started him out again, drove eleven miles and back, with exactly an average of a drink per mile. In addition the buggy carried three big quarts of whiskey for later consumption. Mel's wife was heartbroken.

Looking into his face she said, "I didn't know where you had gone, but if I could have walked through this awful storm I would have searched for you." Mel said he would have given his life if he could have stayed sober, but it wasn't in him.

On another occasion, after a record-breaking period of eleven and one-half sober weeks, Mel succumbed to his vice again, possibly encouraged by a suspended court sentence hanging over him. He went into the country, drove up to a saloon, put the horse in the shed and said, "There's the old nag out there with the buggy. Everybody have something to drink. Drink up the horse!"

"I was just simply imbecile," Mel said later. "There was nothing else to it. And I tried my level best. I don't look like a man that goes down easy, but I just couldn't stop. I went on worse and worse. Finally I got back to the city again; the drunks got oftener and oftener, and they always got a little bit longer.

"For six years I tried to quit. There's no fun in that. Every time after promising my wife and my boy and myself that I'd never take it again, I'd fall. That left me just so much lower in my own estimation; I hated myself. Finally after a drunk I just wouldn't go home any more. I got to staying away for three or four days at first, then a week, and gradually longer and longer. I even committed burglary to satisfy the awful craving for drink.

"They tried to turn me off whiskey, but they didn't have a remedy. You can't tie a big fellow like me with a bit of ribbon. It needs something more than that. They tried the gold cure, and they gave me hypodermic syringes and three bottles of medicine. I sold the whole outfit of stuff in fifteen minutes for three drinks of whiskey.

"God gave us only one baby. When the little fellow was hardly two years old I went to our little home one day—it had almost ceased to be a home—I went home after a ten days' drunk, and found him dead in his mother's arms. I'll never forget that day. I was a slave, and I knew it. It pretty nearly broke my heart. I said, 'I'm a murderer. I'm anything but a man. I can't stand it, and I won't stand it! I'll end my life!' But I didn't have the courage. At my mother's knee I had been taught to say, 'Now I lay me down to sleep.'

I knew there's a God and I didn't dare face Him. I couldn't stand suicide.

"Mrs. Trotter was alone with the little fellow when she laid him down, dead. Then she turned aside to God and said, 'Father, I've had my thoughts on the baby more than on you, and now I want to turn to you. You're all I have left.' Mrs. Trotter had never been away from the baby one hour from the time he was born till he died in her arms. She had a drunken husband, and her only joy and hope was in the baby. And oh, how she cared for him! Then she turned around from the dead child and said, 'Lord, I'm going to serve you, to help others in trouble. I still have my husband.' She began to pray for me. That's a thing that counts; when a wife gets hold of God without letting go, there's something bound to happen.

"She led me into the little room and closed the door upon the three of us. Over the body of our dead baby, lying in the little white casket, she made me promise that I'd never take another drop. I promised, put my arms around her, and told her I'd never touch liquor again as long as I lived. The funeral hadn't been over two hours before I staggered home so drunk I couldn't see. I couldn't help it; the devil had me. Tobacco was just as much a fiend for me as whiskey. My right hand was filled with 'wet ones,' and my left hand pocket with 'dry ones.' "

On the night of January 19, 1897, ragged and drunk, Mel Trotter staggered through the streets of Chicago bound for Lake Michigan, where he had determined to commit suicide by jumping into the icy waters. He was a slave to liquor. He was without home and friends, bound hand and foot by sin. Whiskey had been his god for years. He had tried as few men to get away from it; resolution after resolution failed; promise after promise was broken. He had given up in despair, had left his home and wife, and now had reached the final determination to end everything.

This night when he resolved to plunge into the lake was the darkest in his entire life. He would have given anything for the power of becoming a new man, but he was convinced there was no help.

As he staggered along Van Buren street in his uncertain course, he staggered also into Pacific Garden Mission. The doorkeeper helped him inside, and put him in a chair along the wall so he would not tumble.

Harry Monroe, who had succeeded to the mission superintendency in 1892, was leading singing up on the platform. Seeing the ushers place the ragged drunk against the mission wall, he stopped and asked the crowd to bow in prayer.

"O God," he prayed, "save that poor, poor boy."

Mel Trotter was then twenty-seven years of age. Monroe had been exactly the same age in 1880 when he wandered into the mission. He gave his testimony that night, telling how he had trod a rough road, but how Christ had forgiven him.

At the close of the service, Monroe gave the invitation. "Jesus loves you," he said to the men in the mission, "and so do I. He wants to save you tonight. Put up your hand for prayer. Let God know you want to make room for Him."

Mel Trotter raised his hand for prayer, jumped to his feet and walked forward. Monroe led him to Christ.

From that day forward the two men were great buddies. Harry called Mel his "Timothy" and Harry was "Paul" to Mel. The waters of Lake Michigan were colder than usual that night, but Mel's heart was really warm for the first time. He was headed not for the lake, but for the pulpit. He had tasted Living Water.

## CHAPTER VIII

## A CRADLE OF AMERICAN EVANGELISM

During the years 1880 to 1912 when Monroe proclaimed Christ's redemptive love at Pacific Garden Mission as convert, song leader, assistant superintendent and then superintendent, the historic refuge became a growing cradle of American evangelism.

Folks who slept in cheap flophouses—railroadmen, harvesters, lumbermen, boatmen, longshoremen—were among the best candidates for the ministry that Monroe could find. They came in great numbers to hear his story, and they saw many of their own number go out to preach the Gospel.

Six years before Colonel Clarke died, the mission doors swung open in 1886 to make way for Billy Sunday, but the Colonel did not live to see the trail of heavenly fire with which the ex-baseball star ran the bases from one key city to the next. Sunday's peak came from 1910 to 1920, although he had many campaigns before and after those years.

Likewise, when Mel Trotter was converted in 1897, Colonel Clarke had been dead five years, and nobody dreamed that the mission convert's influence would plant rescue centers in more than one hundred cities.

But Billy Sunday and Mel Trotter were not the only miracles of grace in Pacific Garden Mission annals. True enough, they shook the cradle of American evangelism like few men before or since, but apart from them the steady stream of converts that has gone from the Mission into Christian service has left a tremendous mark upon the nation. When the Clarkes began their venture, Jerry McAuley had the only other rescue mission in the land. Today there are more than two hundred such missions, with five hundred or more full-time workers. Most of them are spiritual children of the first two efforts. Still it has not been only to down-and-outers that Pacific Garden Mission graduates have ministered. In every avenue of Christian service and on every level of human life they have proclaimed the Gospel. Conversion in a mission did not limit their ministry to down-and-outers; other qualifications determined their respective places of service.

The Clarkes had won no insignificant number of converts in the two and one-half years before Harry Monroe walked into the mission. Nor were these converts slow in getting into Christian service. Joe McVeigh, lanky printer, proof-reader and prize-fighter, was only one among many. He had staggered into the mission where Colonel Clarke put his arms around McVeigh's dirty neck and said, "Jesus will save you." McVeigh deserted the heavy drinkers who were his buddies, gave his testimony at every opportunity, and became a Presbyterian preacher in Oregon.

Then came Harry Monroe's powerful testimony. In the years of his ministry the mission was destined to be a seminary graduating Christian workers almost every night with a special B. A. (born again) degree. They had more zeal than knowledge, nobody questions that, but with what knowledge they had the converts in turn went out in the power of Christ and won a great multitude for the kingdom.

There was "Curly" Tom Mackay of Erie, Pennsylvania, born in the shadow of his father's saloon, the Shamrock House. At the age of twelve Tom was shifting for himself, driving mules on the canal. Then he worked for a circus, and later became a jockey. Whiskey sent him askew, and to Chicago where the levee became his stamping ground. He could neither read nor write, but he knew most of the tricks used by hoodlums and gangsters. As a drunken carpenter about to commit a crime—few people know what it was, but Tom said later that "I would have been hanged for it"—he was overtaken by a tract distributor for the mission. Tom was spending the early part of the evening panhandling, already full of liquor. "You don't need soup; you need Jesus," said the mission worker. "Go inside and let Him save you." Tom thought he would at least see what was going on inside. He listened for a while, then fell asleep on the shoulder of a colored man seated next to him. He woke up for the invitation and gave his life to Christ. That was in 1894. He became a mighty voice for God as superintendent of Los Angeles' Helping Hand Mission, and one of the most noted open-air preachers on the Pacific coast.

There was Jacob C. Dudley, born in the blue-grass region of Kentucky where folks raise children and horses. His Virginia grandfather had squandered a fortune in two years on the race course. His losses included thirty negroes that had belonged to his young wife when he married her. If the gambling instinct was hereditary, it skipped Dudley's father, for the lad was reared in a Christian home. From the age of ten Dudley's mind was filled with ideas of the turf. He read all the racing journals, and talked to anyone who knew anything about horses. He almost broke his father's heart when he came home drunk at sixteen, but it was poker that ensnared him like a vise. Dudley spent so much time over the card table that a breakdown resulted which sent him to a tuberculosis sanitarium for over a year. Dudley's Christian wife was heartbroken, but she loved him so tenderly that he became anxious to please her. He joined a church, though he had had no change of heart. During revival meetings, the speaker mentioned some of the changed lives wrought by rescue mission work, among them that of Harry Monroe. So impressed was Dudley that he surrendered all his sins; all, that is, except horse-racing. Soon he had squandered all the money inherited from his father, his salary as secretary of the turf association being his only support.

In September, 1909, he came to Chicago, and early one Sunday night went to Pacific Garden Mission. Only two or three men had arrived. They were eagerly talking about Tom Mackay's conversion. When later the mission became filled and the testimonies were given, Dudley was strangely stirred. When the invitation was given, Dudley was the first to go forward. At the altar he fell on his knees and cried, "O God, here goes everything—race track, and everything!" Mother Clarke gave him a copy of the New Testament after having written Dudley's name inside. On one cover was stamped: "From one who is praying for you"; on the other the words which Dwight L. Moody so often penned on the flyleaf of Bibles he was asked to autograph: "Sin will keep you from this book; this book will keep you from sin." Dudley left the mission that night with the determination to make up the squandered years with "the fag-end of my misspent life." By 1912 he was a city missionary, and later was in charge of the rescue mission in Memphis, Tennessee.

There was A. E. Nissen, Iowa businessman. Stunned by the death of his wife, and almost insane with distress, he could find no cure for his loneliness until he wandered into the mission and found Christ. He gave up his business and became a Salvation Army Soldier.

There was Dick Lane, with a forty-year criminal record and stretches in several penitentiaries for burglary and safe blowing. When Dick landed in Chicago the police told him that twenty-four hours in the city would be too long for him to stay. Dick called an old friend and asked for work, saying he was tired of crooked life. With some reluctance Chicago's *Record-Herald* put him to work as a receiving clerk. The following week while passing Pacific Garden Mission curiosity dragged him inside. He had heard preachers tell the Gospel story in jail, but now he heard gangsters telling it from the pulpit. He recognized one of the men giving his testimony as a chap who had served time at Jackson, Michigan, when he was there, so he knew the testimonies were "on the level." When the invitation was given, Dick raised his hand. He felt overpersuaded to go forward, and at the altar pledged his life to Christ. Night after night as a firm soldier for Christ he testified in missions, churches, and on street corners. He stayed with the *Record-Herald* as a trusted employee until death took him in 1913. He left a fiery trail of Christian service.

There was "Sunshine" Harris, steeped in sin for seventy-one years and most of that time an infidel. Leaving home because he was such a disgrace to his family, he wandered around the country. He never went to church except for a funeral, unless to ridicule what took place. For fifty years he smoked and drank, then became such a slave of tobacco that he picked up stubs in the street to satisfy the craving. Filthy with sin he wandered often into the mission, usually drunk, each time resisting the pleadings of Colonel and Mrs. Clarke with scorn and mockery, and determining never to return. On August 4, 1899, he bought a New Testament, hardly knowing why. When his eyes fell upon the words, "Thou fool, this night thy soul is required of thee," he became furious and closed the book. Later he wanted to reread the passage but could not find the verse. That made him more furious. In vexation he began with Matthew's genealogy and kept reading until the words were located. A few nights later he said, "God, tonight I am going to the mission. If you help me, I'll raise my hand for prayer." It was a never-to-be-forgotten night for "Sunshine" Harris.

"When the invitation was given I looked at one hand and it was so black and sinful, and then at the other and that was just as bad, so I raised both hands and was assisted by a Christian lady to the altar," he wrote, "and when I called upon the Lord He heard my cry, and the load of sin, mountain high, rolled off, and I rose to my feet and exclaimed, 'Thanks be to God for his unspeakable gift, and for Pacific Garden Mission.' " Harris sponsored an unscheduled housecleaning in his filthy little room that night. Whiskey and beer bottles, old pipes and tobacco, disgusting pictures, cards and other habilaments of sin went into the furnace, and on the table by his favorite chair he placed instead the New Testament with a slip of paper marking the verse, "Thou fool, this night thy soul is required of thee." Somebody named him "the miracle of the mission." He served God with such spiritual fervor and delight that the mission workers called him "Sunshine" Harris. He loved everybody and everybody loved him, with just one note of exception: during the first weeks of his Christian experience he kept waking during the night and shouting "Glory!" until some of the nearby roomers complained. He moved to other quarters. Night after night he continued to testify at the mission, eager to tell how the Lord had cleaned his life. When he died June 10, 1907, he said in his cheerful optimism, "Tell them at the Mission I am going home to glory in the good, old-fashioned way." So clearly had his testimony rung out on Van Buren street among the drink and tobacco addicts that once were his companions, that when Harris' body was buried at Elburn, Illinois, all the hoboes on the levee knew his soul had gone to God.

There was Robert Atchison, who was picked out of Chicago's slums in 1893 and went out from the mission as a missionary to the Orient and became known as the "Mueller of Japan," and the "Mikado." Drink so overpowered him that he would sell his clothes for liquor. He became a tramp, riding freight cars to Florida when the cold north weather was too penetrating for his scanty clothing. He had been hired and fired by most of the railroad companies. He slept in deserted houses and begged meals and handouts at back doors. For nearly fifteen years he felt impelled to walk inside the Pacific Garden Mission. There he heard the story of the cross. The next night he returned and was saved. His first job was to make restitution to a Brooklyn woman to whom he owed forty dollars for board. She replied, "I am very glad of the change in your life, and very glad to receive the money as I need it." Ten years later, Atchison, his wife and two children, sailed for Japan, without any human sponsorship, but with Philippians 4:19—"my God shall supply all your need according to His riches in glory by Christ Jesus"—committed to memory. Eighteen years they travelled through the mountains and valleys of Japan, over twenty-five hundred miles on foot to spread the Gospel in remote places. A diet of rice and fish was their sustenance. Once they were rescued from a furious mob about to stone them for preaching Christ in their village. Another time, while the black plague swept hundreds to death around them, Atchison wrote that "we wrapped ourselves up in the ninety-first Psalm and continued about the Lord's business." Atchison often said that when God got through, the devil had made an awful fool of himself. Fifteen years of tramping around the United States with whatever passed for food and lodging was God's training school for missionary service in Japan, "where food was bad and sleeping worse." It was in Kobe, Japan, where Atchison first met Charles M. Alexander, the noted Gospel singer. Learning that the missionary was saved in Pacific Garden Mission, Alexander said, "That's an awful place to get saved in." Then he repeated the statement. "They tell me," he continued, "that a person who gets saved in the Pacific Garden Mission never gets over it." Atchison smiled. "As far as I'm concerned," he said, "you surely struck the nail on the head."

There was Edward Card, railroad express messenger, who lost his job for chronic drunkenness. Walking into the mission, he met Harry Monroe, and was converted. He went to St. Louis and founded the Sunshine Mission. At Mel Trotter's annual mission conference in Grand Rapids, Card and Harry Monroe almost annually would rise to sing together, "There's Glory in My Soul."

There was F. M. Smith, "the man at the prison gate." Before the Clarkes had ever founded Pacific Garden Mission, he had drifted into sin. Liquor, dope and crime had all left their scars before Smith reached Blackwell's Island, and then jail after jail. He sank so low that not a single relative or friend recognized him. In 1896, as an inmate in Cook County jail, he heard a Gospel team from the Moody Bible Institute. The selfsame day Mrs. Clarke stopped for a moment at his cell and offered the first "mother's prayer" Smith had ever heard. The following Sunday Mother Clarke came again, put her hand through the cell bars, resting it on the prisoner's head while she prayed for him. As soon as she had gone, Smith threw himself on the stone floor and prayed to God for mercy. A heavenly joy flooded his soul that moment. A few days later he went on trial, pleaded guilty, and was sentenced to three years in Joliet. Having lived with his Bible. he was pardoned in less than half that time. He spent his days at Moody Bible Institute and his nights at Pacific Garden Mission, where Mother Clarke and Harry Monroe helped and encouraged him. Then, removing to Philadelphia, he became head of an office furniture manufacturing enterprise, and for more than a quarter century proclaimed the glad tidings of redemption as a Christian layman.

There was George Preston, the prayers of whose mother reached from north Ireland across the sea. For twenty years Preston, a gifted singer, was on the operatic and theatrical stage in Europe, Canada and the United States. On Sunday afternoon, September 25, 1910, while walking down State street in Chicago, Preston saw the mission's gospel wagon. Drawn by two horses, the black carriage had a high roof and open sides. In it were a half dozen men with musical instruments, and around the carriage a half dozen others, talking and singing. There was a big crowd at the corner. Preston stopped to listen to the music. Then Harry Monroe began speaking. Preston was quite disinterested until he heard Monroe say, "I am impressed that there is a man here who has been thinking that years ago he promised his mother he would meet her in heaven." Almost immediately Preston shouted: "I am that man!" Pushing his way through the crowd, he stepped to the mission group, knelt by the wagon wheel and asked Jesus to save him. Until his death in 1941 he told redemption's story as an evangelist and singer.

There was John F. Wendell, whose love of liquor reduced him to poverty. Repeatedly he was housed in a cell for drunkenness at the Harrison Street police station directly across the street from the little flat where lived his wife and children. Wendell sought treatment for delirium tremens, but his physician finally lost patience, saying, "Let him die like a dog." On November 19, 1893, a bitter cold night, with not a penny in his pocket, he wandered into Pacific Garden Mission as an alternative to begging. There he met Jesus Christ face to face and was converted. Often he returned to the mission to give his testimony, and prompted many to repentance and belief in Christ.

There was Billy Driver, the Scotchman, whose trade as carpenter was the only thing he had in common with Jesus Christ. A victim of drink and vice, he found new life at Pacific Garden Mission and then went to Denver, Colorado. There he worked at his trade during the day, and at his own expense kept up a mission at night. It developed into Denver's Sunshine Mission. After some years, Driver became an evangelist, serving faithfully until his death in 1927.

There was Lew Speegle, the street fakir, whose checkered career carried him apart from his wife and family in California, and sent him around the world as a drifter and steerer for clairvoyants, pickpockets and other crooks. One warm Sunday afternoon he was selling dime articles to the passing crowds at State and Harrison. Soon the Mission's gospel wagon drew alongside on its weekly "fishing trip" and stopped near the crowd. Speegle resented the invasion. He decided to abandon the spot to the "religious cranks," but the gospel music seemed to grip his heart. Men told how Christ saved them from the depths of sin and then came Harry Monroe's warm invitation. Speegle resisted and slipped away. Even in Mexico, his next stop, he could not forget the invitation nor escape the conviction that he should receive Christ as Savior. He jumped a north-bound freight train, determined to find the men who spoke that day about Christ's power to save. After quite a search he found the old mission and when the opportunity came, knelt in prayer and found Christ. The next day he went to work and made the first honest money in years. Night after night he returned to the mission to give his ringing testimony and then enrolled at Moody Bible Institute to prepare for practical Christian work. Some time later, the mission workers found him in an unhappy mood. They learned of sinful chapters in his past life that had never been righted, and prompted him to make restitution. Speegle wrote nineteen letters of confession, in which he admitted taking money unlawfully. Another went to the United States Navy, confessing desertion. As a result, he was arrested by the government, taken to Washington for a hearing, and faced with loss of citizenship and time in Leavenworth, the usual sentence. When the stern naval officers heard his stirring testimony they told him to go back into the service and finish out his term. He soon had a Bible class under way in the town near his vessel. Before half his term was completed, he was given his liberty. From there with an old automobile, he toured the state of Ohio, preaching and distributing tracts. Then he became evangelist in Wisconsin, at the same time carrying on his business in order to pay the last of the old debts that weighed upon him. When his business moved him to Chicago, he returned faithfully to the mission to give the story of God's redemptive power.

There was Martin O'Connor, the plumber's assistant, who couldn't take care of the leak that made him so thirsty for whiskey. It was in a drunken stupor that he found himself one night at Pacific Garden Mission. There he was, sunk in the depths of sin, with the added burden of tuberculosis to remind him of his waywardness. At the close of the service, the evening's speaker, Mr. Calverley, took O'Connor by the hand and led him to the altar. Kneeling beside him was Mother Clarke, speaking the first words of Gospel love that he had ever heard in his life. "My friend, your trouble is not whiskey, or tobacco, or bad habits, or bad companions, or hard luck. Your trouble is sin. Sin separates you from God, and if you die in this condition, you will be separated from Him forever." Then came precious words to the soul of Martin O'Connor. "But God loves you and wants to save you from sin and the penalty of sin, so He sent His son Jesus into the world to take your place, and die in your stead. If you will take Him as your Savior, God will not only forgive your sins, but will give you the power to live a life of victory over them." Then she prayed. He left the mission that night trusting God to keep him. The very next morning found O'Connor beginning to enter a saloon. The appetite for whiskey was gone, however. God had not failed. His attendance and testimony at the meetings were faithful. About five weeks after his conversion Harry Monroe asked O'Connor to be "Custodian" at the mission. As Martin O'Connor said, "Although this was to be a temporary arrangement, I stayed on the job and for six years was known as 'Harry's right hand man.' Mrs. Clarke's office was my home and through the lives of her and Mr. Monroe, I was very much encouraged and received many valuable lessons." In 1914 O'Connor took over the South State Street Mission for eight years, or until the Pacific Garden Mission moved to its present location. Then came a call to northern Wisconsin where now for over fifteen years this vessel of God's grace and his wife have been preaching the matchless Word of Life to countless souls.

There was John Troy, grandson of a wealthy Serbian sea-merchant, and son of a famous European physician and law-maker. But here he was, adrift in Chicago, far from family and friends, penniless, and unable to speak English. It was a sorry state for one who had enjoyed many privileges. One night in the winter of 1907-1908 he walked into Pacific Garden Mission. It was the first Protestant service he had ever attended. Unable to understand the language, he nevertheless sensed the radiance and joy that welled from the hearts of the speakers. He wanted what they had. Staying to talk with Harry Monroe and the workers after the meeting the best he could, Troy was told the story of Jesus' love. By the time summer came he was in a way able to understand what Christ could do for him. On the last Sunday night of August, 1908, he accordingly responded to the invitation and accepted Jesus Christ as Savior. In 1915 he was graduated from the Moody Bible Institute and since that time has been engaged in evangelistic work in America, Canada, Great Britain, and the European continent. As John Troy himself has said, "Truly our God is a miracle worker, and I praise Him for the Pacific Garden Mission where I first heard the Gospel."

There was John Lester Osborne, who left home at seventeen and lived almost twenty years in sin and drink. When he awakened one Sunday morning, under the influence of liquor, he heard his son in the kitchen quoting Matthew 11:28. The words gripped his heart for a time, but again he fell into sin. The only solution seemed to lie in taking his life. On the night of November 11, 1894, however, he wandered into the mission, walked down the middle aisle, sat down on the end chair in the third row from the front, bowed his head and prayed to God for help. From that time on, he became an usher in the mission and drove the team of horses on the Gospel wagon. These drivers felt they, too, had a divine commission for Gospel work, based on Luke 14:21: "Go quickly into the streets and lanes of the city and bring in hither the poor and the maimed and the halt and the blind." Osborne later attended Moody Bible Institute, and for twenty-four years continued in the employ of that school.

There was Elias Auger, who in 1899 drifted into Chicago from Massachusetts, without friends, money or God. He was converted in the mission, and became a Baptist minister and chaplain, enjoying more than thirty years of Christian service after completing his theological studies.

There was that almost inseparable gospel song team, Mott and McCoy. Mott, a Canadian, was converted at the mission under Mother Clarke's influence in 1885. Nevertheless he fell back into drinking and gambling and narrowly escaped being murdered. When he came back to the fold he found McCoy, a Hoosier, whose talent and prosperity had become his ruin. McCoy was a fine tenor, and had sung in many exceptional choirs, including that of the Mormons in the Salt Lake City temple. But drink had got the better of him, too, and his life was being spent in Chicago's south Clark street barrel-houses as fiddler. Around 1910 he went to the mission on a Sunday morning and heard Tom Beaumont, the carpenter convert, give a Bible talk. He took Christ as his Savior. McCoy, however, fell back into sin. Ten years after his first profession of Christ he was walking down State street when the gospel wagon came along. Mott spotted him; Walter Taylor, the mission superintendent, singled him out. "Come here, McCoy," Taylor shouted. "I want to congratulate you." McCoy wandered up sheepishly. "You and Mott used to sing together," said Taylor, "do it now." McCoy shook hands with Mott. They sang a Gospel song and McCoy was reunited with Christ.

There was Arvilla Beardsley, who left her small town home at seventeen for the glitter and jazz of the big city. She played her squeaky violin in a cabaret and soon reveled in night life with zest and abandon. Soon, however, despairing of life, she walked into the mission on January 25, 1911, just as Mrs. Ralph Norton of the Belgian Mission was singing "You Must Do Something Tonight." Arvilla yielded her heart to God and returned for many years to the old rescue house to play her violin to the glory of God.

There was Charlie Palmer, a well-known harness dealer. He picked a strange night to jump into the waters of Lake Michigan. Above him, the waning moon peered dimly through jagged, wind-blown clouds. The waves roared against the stone walls of the breakwater. Along the shore stood the solitary figure of Charlie Palmer, struggling to make up his mind. Born into a good family that gave him religious training, he nevertheless enjoyed quibbling with members of his home church, and finally joined an infidel club, of which he became a blatant enthusiast. Then came the craze for gambling. His wife could stand it no longer. Finally, joining hands with her over the crib of their sleeping baby, Palmer pledged never to enter another gambling hall. When he broke the oath, he cut a vein in his wrist, dipped a pen into the flowing blood, and wrote out another pledge. It worked no better. His wife finally left him. Palmer often went at dusk to the suburban town where she lived, stationed himself across the street and watched the shadows on the window blind as the mother held their child in her arms. Then, his eyes flowing with tears, he would return to the city, go to some gambling den and play the wheels.

One night he went to Pacific Garden Mission, simply because he had nothing else to do. He heard Dick Lane testify how God had taken the love of gambling out of his heart. He went back again to hear Lane repeat the story. The second time Palmer followed Lane home from the mission, to make sure Lane didn't stop in at a gambling hole along the street. For forty-two nights in succession he trailed Lane to his house in similar fashion. Convinced that Lane had the real thing, Palmer began to despair for himself, for he stood the more convicted of his own bankrupt life. It was now the night he found himself walking along the lake shore. There was some comfort in the thought that with a single plunge he could end his mental torture. Lifting his hands to heaven he cried to God for help. Something suddenly changed within him. He knew Christ had heard his petition and washed his sins away. He went back to the mission and gave his testimony. His next move was to find Mrs. Palmer and their child. She welcomed him with open arms, and their home became a cathedral. Palmer entered business, and to the end held high his Christian testimony as a workman and as an early member of the Gideons. When the hour of death came and he lapsed into unconsciousness, he prayed for the faithful workers who carry the testimony of Christ's redeeming grace to needy men and women.

The growing army of mission converts spilled over the nation. The largest proportion did not enter full-time Christian service in the sense of giving up secular employment, but the converts showed remarkable persistence and growth. From the beginning the mission's objective was to turn every convert into a missionary, whether in full-time Christian service or not. So it was that a tremendous lay witness was created, and as the years passed, almost every great firm in Chicago knew first hand the story of some drifter who had been on the verge of suicide, but had found Christ at the mission and was now making good.

Such was the work of Pacific Garden Mission in its earlier years, when, as today, it cradled American evangelists. They did not all step from the mission to the pulpit, though many did. But they stepped from the devil's stamping ground to God's trail for lost men, and in so doing, held the torch of faith aloft so others, too, could find the way.

CHAPTER IX

# THE GREAT TRIUMVIRATE

Towering above those lesser lights in the early years of the twentieth century, however, were three men in particular: Harry Monroe, Mel Trotter and Billy Sunday. More than any others of that generation, they held aloft the story of the cross as living examples of the ministry of Pacific Garden Mission. They served God individually with mighty power and, when their paths came together in service, formed a great triumvirate.

Harry Monroe, as almost everybody knows, had a part in bringing Trotter and Sunday to Christ. But too often his outreach has been measured by those conversions only. Monroe was the secret confidante of the hoodlums of State street as well. Twenty-four hours before some crimes were committed he could have informed the police of pending events. Often he pleaded with men for hours not to carry through their plans, but rather to surrender to Christ. Small-time gangsters came to the old mission to hear some of their former associates testify, would struggle with Christ only to spurn Him again, and when Harry Monroe invited them to come to Jesus, would say something like, "Sorry, Harry, but we've got a job to do on the west side tonight."

Harry held their respect, and, hoodlums though they were, they wanted to shoot straight with him. They were the group that made the mission work doubly difficult, however, because word sometimes spread that the place was a shelter for criminals. But it wasn't. Harry Monroe preached his heart out against crime and sin of every sort. When gangsters were present, he presented his star witnesses for testimony, and glad they were to tell how Christ had changed their twisted lives. They led lawbreakers to the very brink of hell and to the very brink of heaven, then gave them their choice. Monroe poured his heart into the invitation and when men came through to Christ, they truly came from the depths of sin to the heights of victory.

The old timers still remember Harry as "the dean of the mission." Nothing ever went wrong but that he was master

Clarke always thought God would some day use Mel at the mission. For six months in 1912 Mel took over the mission entirely, then entrusted it to assistant superintendents, nevertheless remaining in general charge for six years.

It was in December, 1915, when Harry Monroe was on a nation-wide tour with Mel Trotter that he broke down completely and was taken to the Hinsdale sanitarium, the Presbyterian hospital, and then to Wisconsin. In July, 1916, he was taken to his Morgan Park home where, two weeks later, on the last day of the month he died at the age of sixty-three. It was a deep time of sorrow at the old mission when Thomas J. Marx, a converted Catholic pullman company employee, and acting mission superintendent, made the announcement. Monroe's wish had been that Paul Rader, noted Christian and Missionary Alliance evangelist, should preach the funeral sermon, but Rader was prevented from complying because of large meetings he was holding on the west coast. When Monroe's body was laid to rest in Mount Greenwood Cemetery, where Colonel Clarke had gone to his grave before him, they did not realize that in addition to his zealous record of service, Monroe in his will left the mission one thousand dollars to be charged against his real estate. Monroe was too busy winning souls to acquire what he had hoped, however. At a meeting of the mission trustees in 1919, Mel Trotter offered a motion, unanimously accepted, that:

> WHEREAS, it appears that upon the death of Harry Monroe his estate was not possessed of any real estate, and was possessed of but comparatively little personal property, and it further appearing that such personal property would hardly suffice for the comfortable support of his widow,
>
> NOW, THEREFORE, BE IT RESOLVED, that Pacific Garden Mission shall release and waive, and it does hereby release and waive, any and all claims which the said Pacific Garden Mission might or could have against the estate of Harry Monroe, deceased, resulting from, pertaining to, or growing out of the terms of the will of the said Harry Monroe, deceased.

With the death of Harry Monroe, the acting superintendency fell to Bob Ingersoll, who served for two years until 1918, that fateful year in which Mother Clarke died, the year which was destined to bring to the mission a superintendent who would stay at the State street haven for eighteen years, a man that Mel Trotter felt would make a worthy successor to Harry Monroe. He was right.

Mel Trotter's service propelled him all over the country. His love of the Bible and his passion for men endowed him with two unbeatable qualities for an evangelist.

He had begun his family altar with a portion of the New Testament that cost three cents. "I didn't know where to begin," he said, "so I started to read in Matthew and the names got me up a tree before I finished the second verse. In the next chapter it got better. Then I got down on my knees and prayed the best I knew how. Presently I began reading the New Testament on the street car. You couldn't ride a car seven miles from town and read a Testament and let a lot of women stand while you sat down. Standing or seated, I memorized verses, and the first year I had three hundred and sixty-five verses in my head, and what is better, in my heart." He didn't read a newspaper for two years after his conversion. (His favorite Scripture verse was II Corinthians 5:17.)

Trotter made $4.20 the first week after he was saved. Out of that, his wife gave him sixty cents for carfare and took a dollar a week for rent. Nor did she complain. "I'd rather live in one room and have Mel sober," she said, "than live in a palace with a drunkard." Before Mel finished, he had paid back $1,800 of indebtedness.

During those early days Mel went to work in the barber shop run by his brother, Bill, who had been converted several years before and who played the old organ for Mother Clarke. Bill put Mel on customers he knew wouldn't kick if he cut them slightly. Mel's hand shook so much from drink that he thought he could never shave anybody.

Mel spent every night in Pacific Garden Mission, where he strummed the guitar a bit and sang Gospel songs. He often sang with Harry Monroe, and together they went out to Chicago area churches as a Gospel team.

In January, 1900, at the invitation of businessmen in Grand Rapids, Monroe took some mission converts to that city to tell them the value of rescue mission work. In that party was Mel Trotter, never dreaming that he would spend most of forty years in that city. Eleven hundred dollars was raised to start a Grand Rapids work. A month later the effort was begun in an unoccupied store. To the surprise of everyone, Trotter was chosen the new superintendent, though he had never led a mission meeting in his life. He was "scared stiff," he said, when on the first night he found more women present than men, especially since he had the questionable gift of excessive slang. That very night, however, three young women were saved. One became a missionary, one married a preacher, and the other worked faithfully in the mission for years. Mel Trotter knew God's hand of approval had rested on what was destined to become the largest rescue mission in the world. Mel told his story in a gripping autobiography, *These Forty Years.*

During Billy Sunday's earlier years of preaching, when he was practicing his sermons with good success on Iowa and Illinois congregations, he often sent for Mel for the last night of a campaign. Mel's testimony thrilled multitudes. When Sunday went ahead to the next campaign, Mel stayed behind to care for the converted men and to help them start small missions. In this way, rescue work was organized in many small cities in Illinois and Iowa, among them Jacksonville, Decatur, Springfield, Kankakee, Galva, Galesburg and Bloomington. When Billy took sick in Memphis and was faced with two or three weeks of meetings, he called Mel to take over for him. The folks liked Mel as much as his predecessor. Fat and pudgy, Mel was a kindly soul, with a real modesty. He never talked about the success of his meeting or the number of souls that were saved. He quoted Scripture at length, and whenever friends saw him after a period of absence, they knew that Mel was constantly growing spiritually.

In a setting similar to Pacific Garden Mission environment, the Mel Trotter Rescue Mission was snuggled among saloons, several red light districts, flophouses, a burlesque theater where liquor was served to patrons during the performance, and other notorious enterprises. The hoodlums were certain they could frighten Trotter away, but they discovered he had a muscular Christianity, too. But more than once his victims returned to the mission for the other kind.

It was Mel who introduced the gospel wagon to Grand Rapids, driving it to various street corners and parks for outdoor meetings, as Harry Monroe had done for Pacific Garden Mission. Jail visitation also became a prominent feature of the Michigan mission.

Besides his own mission, with its 1,500 seating capacity, Mel founded sixty-six other Gospel lighthouses in such cities as Milwaukee, South Bend, Muskegon, Kalamazoo, St. Paul,

Pittsburgh and Los Angeles. His two brothers. who with Mel had been drunkards and once tended bar for their own father. dedicated their lives to Christ also. One. George opened a mission in Saginaw. Michigan. and the other. Will, in Los Angeles. Mel traveled all over the country, training local men. some of them former derelicts, to superintend these establishments. He was "Everlastingly At It," as the motto of his mission set forth.

His evangelistic work carried him around the world. He made respectable contacts of every sort and used them to further the work. He held membership in Chicago's Union League Club. Rotary International, and the Tuna Club of Avalon. California

He returned to Pacific Garden Mission as often as he could, considering his tremendous travel and his duties at Grand Rapids. "The Pacific Garden Mission means everything to me." Mel said. "I consider it the brightest spot in all Chicago. Every time I go to Chicago the first place I start for is the old mission. and find the spot on the altar where Jesus spoke peace to my soul." He was seldom without converts on his visits to the mission.

When Mel appeared before a Presbytery meeting to undergo an examination to determine his qualifications for ordination as a Gospel minister, he faced some probing questions but rose to the occasion. One answer came with such trigger quickness that the Presbytery was nonplussed until Mel explained it. "What do you believe about doctrine, Mr. Trotter?" he was asked. "I believe in the 'Monroe Doctrine,'" Mel answered. "I got it straight from Harry himself."

One night Mel's testimony won another barber. Edward Coulson. for the Lord. Given to drink. he lost his job and family. and was desperate when he wandered into the mission that memorable night. As Coulson himself related: "When Mel Trotter got up to give his testimony I was all attention and remember him saying. 'Here stands two hundred pounds of salvation.' and that he had been a barber. He told his story to the glory of God and the salvation of my soul. While I did not surrender my life to God that night. I was the first man to lift my hand for prayer the next night which was September 16. 1902. at nine o'clock." After his conversion Coulson went back to his former employer who promised him a gold watch if Coulson stayed sober for six months Coulson got the watch. Later he opened shops of his own in Chicago and California, using every opportunity to witness to the saving grace of God.

On another night, in October, 1919, Mel spoke at the mission on John 6:37. That night Casey Jones, the baggage smasher, was won to Christ. Jones was born in Greenup, Kentucky, but ran away at an early age to see the world. His first drink of whiskey, in Cuba, made him a drunkard. He spent three years in the army, but left it only a boozehound and gambler. He married, tried to reform by joining a church, but again fell a victim to drink. His various jobs with railroad companies were of short duration, lasting only until the next debauch. Then one day, a conductor on the Chesapeake and Ohio pleaded with Casey to take Christ as Savior, and even took him to meetings where Jones went forward. Several days later, however, drink had again become the master. The night Casey walked into Pacific Garden Mission he heard "Mel preach my life right at me. I grew angry and had picked out a spot on my friend's chin to smack as I was sure he had tipped Trotter off about me." For the invitation Mel said, "If there's a man here who has tried to handle his own life and defeat is staring him in the face, but he really wants to be a man, will he raise his hand for prayer?" Casey did. He went forward and left the mission sure of conversion. Casey began paying old debts, emptied his grip of liquor bottles, cards and dice, and gave his testimony to Christ's saving power far and wide. The railroad officials who detested Casey, soon honored him. He was promoted to conductor, placed upon three different boards in short order, and the officials soon became his best friends. The Chesapeake and Ohio never had a more honored conductor than Casey. From the Atlantic to the Pacific folks wanted to hear his testimony; in jails, prisons, missions, churches, switch shanties, street meetings and hospitals he told what Jesus Christ had done for him. "I tell them the power of Jones, and how helpless he was," he says; "then I tell them the power of Jesus, and what a Savior He is."

In 1937 Mel Trotter sailed to England with Dr. Harry A. Ironside for the Dwight L. Moody centenary celebration. They shared the same cabin on the Aquitania. Before the great multitudes in Westminster's Central Hall, the nightly program listed an outstanding British speaker, followed by Dr. Ironside and Mel Trotter on alternate nights. Aware of the culture of many English audiences, Mel was troubled about his diction, a situation that was helped not at all when

a well-meaning Englishman warned him that American col-
loquialism is not nearly as acceptable on the isles as it is at
home. When Mel first took the platform he was mechanical
and stilted and hardly himself. Finally, realizing that he
was progressing quite unnaturally and quite unsuccessfully,
he stopped nervously for a moment, then remarked that he
had been cautioned about his diction. "I lost three-quarters
of my vocabulary the night I was converted," he said, "and
I have to do the best I can with what I have left." Then he
drove into his message, slang or no slang. "Remember Lot's
wife," he said; "she rubbered and was seasoned forever." The
auditors gasped and gaped. "That's all right," reacted Mel,
"you'll get it by freight—later!" Back in the crowd Mel's
old friend, G. Campbell Morgan, thought he could help breach
the gap. He laughed at the top of his voice; the crowd recognized his laugh and joined in the merriment. From that
moment onward Mel was in stride. He plunged into the
throng and pleaded for souls. Nouns, verbs, adjectives—
Americanisms or no Americanisms—flowed forth calling men
and women to Christ. When the invitation was given, forty
souls responded to the call.

On his spiritual birthday, Mel always arranged a great
annual mission meeting for testimony by converts, at which
time he also made it a practice to tell the story of his own
conversion. In January, 1940, however, he was not at all well,
and it was feared that he would be unable to observe his
forty-third spiritual anniversary in the customary manner.
Since becoming ill on the tour to the British Isles and spending some time in a hospital, he had suffered physically in a
number of ways. He managed, however, to attend the mission service and to speak a few words to the large audience.
It was his last public appearance at the mission.

Mel died Wednesday, September 11, 1940, at his home at
Macatawa Park, near Grand Rapids. The previous April he
was stricken while doing mission work in North Carolina and
never recovered. It seemed for a time as if he might regain
his health. Even under the added strain he faithfully attended
to all mission correspondence, although his assistant superintendent, John Shy, arranged the meetings. The day before
death, Mel was able to go for an automobile ride. The next
morning, as was his custom during the last months, he break-
fasted in bed and remarked that he felt better. An hour later,
when the mission secretary came with the mail, she found

him dead. Seventy years of age, he had risen from the depths of sin to the superintendency of Pacific Garden Mission and to a post on its board of trustees, which he held for many years; he had founded sixty-seven rescue missions, among them the world's largest at Grand Rapids which he directed; he had achieved international reputation as an evangelist. He left no great stone building other than his mission, but he left a trail of converts to Christ that stretched around the world, and that weeded "Hell's Half Acres" out of scores of cities.

When the funeral services were held in the Mel Trotter Rescue Mission in Grand Rapids, the Rev. Homer A. Hammontree, director of music at Moody Bible Institute and for many years an associate with Trotter in evangelistic campaigns throughout the states, presided. Dr. Ironside delivered the message. Among the other speakers was Arthur Blackmore, formerly a Grand Rapids barber and one of Mel's early converts, who went into Christian service and now was superintendent of the City Mission in Erie, Pennsylvania. He represented the International Union of Gospel Missions, an international organization of mission workers, scores of whom traced their spiritual birthdays to the ministry of Mel Trotter. More than a dozen such superintendents were present.

Billy Sunday brought something additional to Pacific Garden Mission prestige. Monroe had lent the mission a thirty-year superintendency with a great personal testimony to God's ability to save from the depths. Trotter demonstrated that same ability in his own life, and helped to make rescue missions almost omnipresent. Billy Sunday made the Pacific Garden Mission a byword in the backwoods of America. He was not limited to a single city, as was Trotter despite his far-flung evangelistic outreach, but rather went up and down the land preaching the Gospel and telling the story of his own conversion.

For thirty-nine years Sunday labored as a nationally-known evangelist, yet he never forgot his spiritual birthplace. "Ma" Sunday as a young Christian knew him as a ball player. When he told her the story of his conversion, she could talk intelligently about the mighty power of God. They were married in 1888.

During those early years, Billy was a familiar figure at the mission. He went there at every opportunity and learned to give his testimony. Although he was a poor speaker, his baseball halo gave him a weighty background for his words.

He stammered and fumbled for words at the Sunday school, Y. M. C. A., and Christian Endeavor meetings where he spoke, just as he did in the mission meetings, but still he was in demand. The heart of his message was the story of his conversion—how he sat on the curbstone, heard the street meeting, came inside the mission, heard Harry Monroe, and later found Christ as Savior. He could think of little else to say and, anyway, that was what the people wanted to hear.

But Billy did not stop there, whether in the mission or elsewhere. He could always add: "Now, how about you? Jesus did it for me; He can do it for you. Will you give Him the chance?" He knew how to do personal work. When he took Helen Thompson, later "Ma" Sunday, to Pacific Garden Mission with him, his mind was on other things than his love for her. He was tremendously concerned about God's love for men. He gave his testimony faithfully and listened eagerly to those of others. Then with an eagle-eye Sunday watched Harry Monroe throw his pitches as he closed in to retire the opponents. Those lessons in drawing the net, and in individual soul-winning as he stayed after the invitation was given Sunday never forgot.

It was Billy's aptness in dealing with men that prompted the Chicago Y. M. C. A. to offer him an assistant secretaryship. "Ma" Sunday's counsel supported Billy in his decision not to accept a physical director's post, but rather to go into the more spiritual aspect of the work. Much of his work was routine, but he was not diverted from a recognition that the basic need was the winning of individuals to Christ.

Sunday's next task, after three years with the Y work, was as advance agent and promotion man for Dr. J. Wilbur Chapman's evangelistic thrust. Thus he learned every phase of local and nationwide evangelism before Chapman stepped out of revivalism in 1896 into a big Philadelphia pulpit. By that time Sunday had enough gleanings for eight sermons, though he could give his testimony on another night, if he were called for a campaign that long. For six days after he parted with Chapman, Billy was in the dark; he had no meetings, no plans. Then, all unexpectedly, came an invitation for a union meeting in Garner, Iowa, where the Baptists, Presbyterians, and Methodists had merged and rented an opera house. Billy stayed eight days, preached all the sermons he knew, and won two hundred sixty-eight souls. From that time he never lacked an invitation to speak. Even when his homiletic ability was fully developed, he never got beyond the simple Gospel message he heard in Pacific Garden Mission.

One needs only to read *Billy Sunday: The Man and His Message* to realize how he shook the very fiber of great American cities for Christ. Every time his train carried him to Chicago and he had an open night in that city, he made his way to the mission to tell his story, though he never gave the message as such without invitation. Harry Monroe and Mel Trotter almost always urged him to the pulpit. Sunday continued the visits whenever possible. His last visit was in later years when Walter J. Taylor was superintendent.

What Billy Sunday saw and heard in the testimonies at Pacific Garden Mission influenced him no little in his hatred for booze. He was one of the most successful foes of the liquor evil in America, and was able to turn community after community dry. Second only to his antagonism to sin was his antagonism for rum.

If when in Chicago he had only a moment or two to do a transient bit of personal work with some drunkard or moral wreck, he gave a one-minute testimony, preached a one-minute sermon, and then urged the candidate for salvation to visit the Pacific Garden Mission.

An example in point were the few words spoken to a down-and-outer during the Chicago World's Fair that set in motion a chain of circumstances spelling new life for George P. Arthur. Sent from New York after mistreating the bank that had employed him for twenty years, Arthur arrived in Chicago in 1893 without a job. He was dismissed by the Pullman Palace Car Company, of which he had become assistant cashier, for drunkenness. For years he had smoked twenty-five cigars a day. Nor could he quite forget the $30,000 he absconded from the New York bank, the first $1,000 of it as a lad of sixteen during his first year's employment. Billy Sunday saw him and urged him to visit the Pacific Garden Mission. On November 19, 1893, Arthur walked into the rescue mission, met Mother Clarke and Harry Monroe, and was one of seventy-five to go to the altar in response to the appeal. He became financial man for the Evansville Rescue Mission, in Evansville, Indiana.

Among Sunday's friends was a brilliant reporter who covered the Chino-Japanese war for the *New York Tribune*. When he returned to the United States after a shipwreck, the *Tribune* wired him to journey across the arid western states and report irrigation prospects. He was a great writer, but also a great drinker. Coming to Chicago he went to work for the *Times,* but lost that job for drinking. Nobody would conscientiously recommend him any more. One winter night he addressed his personal possessions to his father with the attached note: "I've made a miserable failure of this life. I've disgraced you and sent mother to a premature grave. If you care to look for me, you'll find my body in the Chicago River." The parcel dropped in the snow as he leaped to the rail of the bridge, where an alert policeman seized him. The newspaperman begged for release, and told his miserable story. The policeman answered, "I'm not much on religion, but you can still make a big thing out of life. I'll show you to a place that helps people every night, the Pacific Garden Mission, at 100 East Van Buren street." The reporter followed directions, entered the mission, and sat down next to a bum. After the testimonies, he went forward and accepted Christ. Sunday met him some time later in a Chicago elevator, and they talked together of the spiritual birthplace dear to their hearts, and of their common Savior. "He was secretary in the firm of Morgan and Wright, at $175 a month," Sunday said. "A New York paper offered him an associate editorship, but I told him to stay where he was and tell the old, old story. He was a marvelous power for God."

Billy Sunday always had a hearty handshake for a fellow convert of the old mission; he was as sure that the converts there had the real thing as he was sure of his own fold. More than any other man he told around the country what went on in the Chicago refuge. In his great campaigns in New York, Philadelphia, Boston, Cleveland, Detroit, Indianapolis, Chicago and Cincinnati, multitudes heard for the first time of the little mission outpost in Chicago.

But the publicity Sunday gave the mission was not the only evidence of his appreciation. He and "Ma" Sunday came back home whenever it was convenient; sometimes with only a half-hour stopover on the way to their train out of Chicago, Billy seized the opportunity for a testimony. It was never necessary to prod for a word from him.

But more than this, Billy Sunday gave the mission a cash love offering of $42,000 to further the work. That was his largest, but not his only gift. It represented the net income, after expenses were paid, from Sunday's ten-week Chicago campaign. The pledges ran $70,000, but they were not paid in full. Just as in New York the great evangelist gave the net offering of his campaign to the Red Cross, the Y. M. C. A. and the Y. W. C. A., so in Chicago he said, "I can't do less here, and I want the offerings to go to Pacific Garden Mission." The idea was his own. That fund paid two-thirds of the cost of moving the mission headquarters to a far more promising field, its present address. Mother Clarke's bequest to the mission, left in her will after her death in 1918, paid the other third. Before the shift to the new address, the mission had paid a high yearly rental; at 650 South State street it has already saved twenty years of rent at $5,000 a year, more than double the Billy Sunday gift. And there were other gifts, for at the mission's anniversary meetings, Billy came more than once as special speaker, thus helping to raise several thousand dollars for the annual budget at meetings in big churches. Only once did the evangelist turn in an expense account. Once, at Moody Church, Billy raised $4,400 for the mission, while "Ma" Sunday talked to two overflow crowds and raised an additional $280. After Billy went to glory, "Ma" Sunday came along occasionally for the annual meeting to help stimulate financial interest in the mission.

Like Mel Trotter, Billy Sunday served for years on the mission's board of trustees, though unlike Mel, he never felt the call to rescue mission work. His tremendous interest in it, however, is evidenced by the frequent calls he made for Harry Monroe and Mel Trotter to give their testimonies and to organize converts for mission work, as well as by his own affection for Pacific Garden Mission. Because of his far-flung evangelistic efforts, he seldom attended board meetings, and in 1922 requested that he be dropped as a trustee. President A. M. Johnson, acting for the board, sought to persuade him to continue, but Billy felt he was only a figurehead with his necessary absence, so the board accepted his resignation "with reluctance, appreciating all his life, service and spirit has meant to the mission." The same inability to attend board meetings prompted Homer A. Rodeheaver to resign as trustee the following year. In 1924, when Sunday was taken ill, the mission trustees showed that they still considered him one of their number by writing Billy and "Ma" Sunday, extending to them their love and wishes for a speedy recovery, and inviting Sunday to visit and speak at the mission if possible on his next call to Chicago.

One of the mission's proudest mementoes of Billy Sunday

is the grand piano that traveled with him for part of his barn-
storming revivalism. A huge Baldwin concert model, it was
used mainly in the Chicago meetings in 1918, and then donated
to the mission along with the cash receipts. (The Baldwin
company furnished pianos free for Sunday for years.) It still
sees service at the mission every night, and its notes make the
walls throb with spiritual dynamic and electric memories. The
music rack on the piano is broken, an additional reminder of
the Chicago campaign, when a dope-crazed man, under the
influence of drink, tried to tackle Billy Sunday in the taber-
nacle near the lake. In the scuffle that followed, a chair was
thrown and the rack broken.

The noted evangelist of the sawdust trail—which he carried from the northwoods lumber camps to the heart of
America's key cities—died at seventy-two on November 6,
1935. He had been in poor health for six months, but his
death was unexpected. It was hastened, his friends thought,
by the religious unresponsiveness which came upon America
in the wake of World War I, and by the repeal of prohibition.
These factors did not dishearten Billy, for he had little faith
in human nature but an abundant trust in God. He kept his
fire right to the end, and the Lord's day before his death saw
more than thirty converts at an Indiana service.

From the day that Billy Sunday walked out of Pacific Garden Mission, a new man in Christ, more than one million men
and women had shaken his hand, professing that they had received Christ as personal Savior under his preaching, or had
been restored to the fold from which they were prodigals. He
preached to more than eighty million persons.

On the walls of Pacific Garden Mission are pictures, with
accompanying bronze tablets, of Harry Monroe, Mel Trotter
and Billy Sunday. Heart failure took Mel Trotter to heaven,
and it carried Billy Sunday to glory also. They were a great
triumvirate, but they were only three among the thousands
who went from the old Van Buren street mission to tell what
God had done when they answered His call.

## Chapter X

# IN THE SHADOW OF THE MISSION MOTHER

Mother Clarke's tiny chapel in overalls may have been a laughing-stock to the rising tide of modernistic preachers, but it produced candidates for heaven the like of which never came from Bible-forsaking pulpits. Destructive higher criticism was having its hey-day, but at the rescue mission the whole Bible was preached from Genesis through Revelation, and the skeptical divinity school students who came occasionally for observation had much private fault to find with the mission's theology and homiletics. They could have little to say, however, about the twice-born men that only "the old, old story" seemed capable of fashioning.

For thirty-five years after the mission's founding, Mother Clarke was the great heart of love that moved its hands. After the first fifteen years, in 1892, Colonel Clarke died. All the more she felt the challenge to carry on with a double task.

She was a tiny woman, weighing not over eighty-five pounds, and only about four feet ten inches tall. The little pancake hat that looked like a deaconess' bonnet hardly increased her height. In the second-floor mission office where she made toast and tea for lunch in order to save money for the Lord's work, she spent her days praying and dealing with individuals needing spiritual succor.

In one of these interviews she led Mrs. Elizabeth Williamson Bowen to Christ. A Scotch orphan, Mrs. Bowen reached New York and made a living as soloist in a theatrical company until she left them in Indiana "because of things occurring which were not to my ideas of propriety." One day she stepped curiously into Pacific Garden Mission. From the darkened interior came the voice of Dan Barton, asking if she wanted anything. Dan was in the midst of a prayer, and when the stranger answered, "No," he directed her to Room 12 to see Mother Clarke. The women lunched together, and Mrs. Bowen gave her heart to the Lord. Through the years she sang in evangelistic work with Harry Monroe, Mel Trotter and other mission workers, and for more than thirty-five years attended the Saturday night mission services where her daughter, Mrs. Betty Shaw, often played the piano.

The year Colonel Clarke died was followed by great opportunity for expanded mission effort. The Chicago World's Fair left thousands stranded. Men and women from everywhere were without jobs and without money. Many of them for the first time lay down at night on cobblestones with the sky for a canopy. Many slept under the elevated trestles near the mission. Somehow they found money for drink when they had none for food. Each week brought its tragic tales of destitution, despair and suicide. These people, as the mission reached them, were not difficult to touch. Mother Clarke and her helpers worked overtime. She made the mission her very home. For twenty-seven years—almost 10,000 nights—she attended the mission without missing a single meeting and never mentioned it. Then somebody sensed the meaning of it all, and in 1905 the converts gave her a special party of appreciation.

The mission was a neighbor to vice and sin of the worst kind and the toll in broken hearts and ruined lives was enough to bring tears to the coldest eyes. Tears of joy often rolled from the mission mother's cheeks as she praised God for the salvation of human wrecks, but seldom was Mother Clarke so touched as when she heard the story of Jimmy the Rat. A lad of sixteen on an Indiana farm, he had been introduced to opium by a farm hand, and soon was entranced by the weird phantasies that came with the pipe. Three years later he was a contemptible wretch, hiding in dingy places and nicknamed "the Rat" because he made his bedchamber in a long cupboard shelf. A shaking, shrunken, white-faced phantom of the underworld, he soon wandered into a dope den operated by a Mongolian Chinaman, who sold him cocaine not far from the mission, on south Clark street. The business was ostensibly a laundry, with a street-front room lined with packaged shelves, a long counter, and a painted Chinese girl. Upstairs were the kitchen and some sleeping rooms for John Lee and his helpers, who had a thriving dope business there before the Chinese exodus to Archer Avenue. In the basement the dope victims were confined. It was a long, dark room, with only two windows, one at each street entrance, but even these were boarded. The place was dimly lighted by gas jets, revealing the steep, ladder-like stairs to the ground floor. Along one side of the room, in double tiers, were wooden bunks, upon which through the murky darkness a white face would stare from a pillow, then sink back into oblivion. A Chinaman went noise-lessly about, distributing dope. On the floor were mattresses, and upon them, stupefied men and women.

Black hours and agonized nerves were all that remained to Jimmy the Rat. His only heaven was a cessation of torment, and he welcomed heroin, opium, cocaine, morphine—anything that brought forgetfulness.

Then one day in this place of hell, a bulky, red-haired Irishman, evidently a newcomer to the dope world, came gradually out of his dreams. Outside in the street there was singing. "Whist now!" the Irishman exclaimed suddenly. "Listen to the Pacific Garden Mission boys singing in the street."

Jimmy felt something stir in his heart as he heard the words. He had not sung a hymn since he stopped attending a crossroads church in Indiana as an innocent country boy.

The Irishman raved on to himself. "Them's the mission boys, out in the Gospel wagon this fine Sunday afternoon. And me sittin' in a dope house like a haythen Chinee; better I'd quit, or it's too bad fer me," he added, shaking his head solemnly. Jimmy edged his way to the street entrance to hear the singing more distinctly:

> "Though I forget Him and wander away,
> Still He doth love me wherever I stray;
> Back to His dear loving arms would I flee,
> When I remember that Jesus loves me.
> I am so glad that Jesus loves me,
> Jesus loves me, Jesus loves me;
> I am so glad that Jesus loves me,
> Jesus loves even me."

Softly Jimmy unlocked the door, slipped through a small open-ing, and closed it behind him. Not far away was the Gospel wagon and the crowd that had gathered for the singing. On the car platform was a big husky toughy giving his testimony: "This here Pacific Garden Mission crowd prayed me back to a decent life and—"

A hand stretched through the door and Jimmy was pulled back inside and thrown to the concrete floor. A big Chinaman threatened to kill him. Jimmy was insensible, and was pushed back onto his cupboard shelf. The peddler thought they ought to get rid of Jimmy before he "croaked and the police started in-vestigating the dead lobby gow." Not many hours later some Chinamen carried him down a side street, threw him behind a pile of lumber in front of an unfinished building, and disappeared in the rain.

Jimmy never could remember how he got to Pacific Garden Mission. When he entered, the crowd was singing, and the room was filled. The song ended as he closed the door behind him, so he started up the aisle. He held up both hands and called out: "I want somebody to pray for me!"

Mother Clarke quickly stepped from the platform. She put her hand on his arm and led him to a front seat. When she knelt down, he fell to his knees by her side. Mission workers gathered; prayer after prayer was poured out to God.

Back in Indiana Jimmy became a successful, middle-aged farmer with a Christian wife and children. He gave a fervent testimony to God's saving grace, but stopped using the name "Jimmy the Rat" for the sake of his children. They grew up to say, rather, in their family prayers, "Thank God for Pacific Garden Mission where daddy learned to know Jesus."

In 1909, Chicago's new street numbering system went into effect. The mission's address was no longer 100 East Van Buren street, but 67 West Van Buren. The old number had been easy to remember and was therefore well-suited for promotional purposes; but now, thirty years after the mission's founding, almost everybody in the heart of Chicago knew where it was, and had something to say either for or against it. Mother Clarke passed up and down the Loop streets and gave out thousands of small cards, inviting men and women to the services. The cards read:

HOPE FOR ALL WHO ENTER
PACIFIC GARDEN MISSION
67 West Van Buren Street
WONDERFUL TESTIMONIES
*Strangers and the Poor Always Welcome*
Special Song Service 7:30 Every Night

Seldom a night passed but that the old mission was not filled. Bad weather kept people away from the church, but it drove the outcasts inside for shelter, and the mission workers were glad to see them.

Chicago soon became the winter metropolis of hoboland. Tramps rode the rods from many parts of the country, and the mission had a tremendous job to do. Converts were being lifted from the depths; God had sent great helpers, especially Harry Monroe; but there was still an emptiness in the heart of the mission mother. She wrote, in 1910, the following tribute to the memory of Colonel Clarke:

A TRIBUTE
SACRED TO THE MEMORY OF
MY DEAR HUSBAND

This world is very *lonely*, dear,
   Since Paradise has called you there;
No loving *touch*, no words to cheer,
   Nor all my joys and sorrows *share*.

I list in *vain* for the tread of feet,
   And long for a *touch* of the "vanished hand";
But no loving form is it mine to greet,
   Since called to join the Celestial band.

The journey now I tread *alone*,
   Bereft of *all* my loved ones here,
Whom the Lord has gathered round His throne,
   To be forever with Him there.

*Angelic* hosts are hovering near,
   To guard me safely every hour,
But cannot speak those words *so dear*,
   That human lips, can clothe with power.

No one to greet at "*early morn*,"
   No one to say the fond "*good night*,"
No one to meet me at the *door*,
   With *loving* heart and face so *bright*.

The lonely *days*, the *months*, the *years*,
   Are only known to Him on high,
For He who "*bottles all our tears*,"
   Has numbered *every* secret sigh.

I'm coming *soon* to meet you, dear,
   The journey now is *almost o'er*,
A few more *sheaves* to gather here,
   We'll meet up there to *part no more*.

But she carried on courageously, bent on bringing in the sheaves. She spent Sunday mornings regularly, and often week-day mornings, visiting in the jails. From cell to cell she walked, giving messages of hope and cheer. The jailor at Cook County kept a little chair reserved for Mother Clarke's use when she wanted to visit for any length of time in front of a particular cell.

Her record for perfect mission attendance was broken when she fell down the front steps of her Morgan Park home and suffered a fractured ankle. But the most severe blow came in 1912, when she was hurt in an accident that made it impossible for her to continue mission work. While passing through a revolving door of a State street department store, she was knocked down and severely injured when a tall, heavy man pushed the door, not noticing the slight woman ahead of him. She suffered broken hips and internal injuries. This accident necessitated her relinquishing attendance at the mission and compelled the use of crutches.

For the last years of her life, 1916-1918, Mother Clarke was a complete invalid and unable to converse with anyone. Her devoted nurse, Anna Andrews, who had left the bedside only one day in six years, dropped dead suddenly, and the shock was believed to have hastened Mother Clarke's own death, which occurred two weeks later, on January 29, 1918. She was eighty-three years of age. After her private nurse's death, she was moved to the Hinsdale Sanatorium, the mission trustees having unanimously adopted Mel Trotter's motion that she be removed there, and that the mission "secure for her the best room and nurse, and every possible care and attention for her wellbeing and comfort."

Six months before death, Mother Clarke paid her last visit to the mission. She was carried in a chair to the front row, for a Sunday morning Bible class. She was feeble, and had nothing to say publicly. After the meeting old friends filed by and shook hands; few of them could speak a word.

Just as in life the mission mother's great interest was in supporting the soul-saving station, so in death she made a great provision for it. Annually she had given as much as $4,000 to erase the debts accruing in the course of an extended ministry. She herself kept all of the books and handled the money transactions, so that mission workers and friends seldom knew the extent of her giving. But in her will she left everything to Pacific Garden Mission, the estate coming to about $100,000. It was a providential gift, for the list of mission subscribers, most of them making small contributions, numbered only seventy-five. The rent was high, and, in the wake of the World War, prices were up. The mission began to serve meals regularly to the downtrodden after the War, the only payment for a night's lodging and a breakfast of coffee and rolls being previous attendance at the evening service. The by-laws adopted in 1891 when the mission was incorporated gave as the purpose "to hold and conduct religious services, to carry on and conduct public Gospel missions, to furnish food, lodging and assistance to the needy and unfortunate, and to do religious and benevolent work of all kinds." The first group of trustees included J. A. Burhans, S. B. Chapin, Charles E. Coleman, George W. Dixon, George D. Elderkin, A. M. Johnson, John Nuveen, Homer Rodeheaver, Thomas S. Smith, Billy Sunday, Mel Trotter and George D. Webb.

These were years in which the mission could ill afford to lose Mother Clarke. Harry Monroe was taken from service in 1912 also, and the mission was hard pressed for leadership. Mel Trotter's first duties were to his growing Grand Rapids work, but he was asked to become general superintendent of Pacific Garden Mission, with the understanding that the work be carried on by assistant superintendents. Trotter was overseer from 1912 to 1918, coming to Chicago whenever he could do so, but nobody recognized better than himself that the situation was not ideal. During the early years of this period a group of "holy rollers" worked their way into the mission, and it was related that Harry Monroe, having made his way to the mission one night despite his illness, was taken aback when he entered and saw the boisterousness and hilarity, so turned around and went home again.

During those years of compromised leadership, the mission's soul-saving work suffered little, however. There was a great group of consecrated helpers. Beaumont, Beveridge, W. D. Bowen, Calverley, Oates and Roberts were just a few of the men ready to step in and handle meetings, and the Moody Bible Institute assigned student workers to help. There was much musical talent also, including the familiar names of Bert Bowen, Gillion, Hickey, Foster Mansfield, Marx, Mott, Putnam, Shaw, Wood; Miss Burell, Miss Gordon, Mrs. Bowen and Mrs. Fletcher. The converts who came faithfully to tell the story of Jesus' love were beyond number; Briscoe, Ramey, Wendell and the other old-timers were often with the Gospel wagon or in the mission.

One of the converts—August 14, 1915, was his spiritual birthday—was Bill Hadley, later given charge of the information desk at Moody Bible Institute. Raised in a Christian family, he nevertheless began drinking, and whiskey became his downfall. He lost his job, and soon was a cocaine as well as alcohol addict. Safebreaking, picking pockets, and hold-ups supplied money for dope, and even a gold crown from a tooth provided the means for several drinks. Arrested four times in Dayton, Ohio, the police chief gave him one hour to leave the city. Two terms in the Bridewell followed. During the "Pan American" exposition in Buffalo, he held up a postal clerk and was given a long penitentiary term. Then he went to the Chicago underworld, and later to Cook county jail. After leaving confinement there, he staggered back to the old dens, got in trouble in a whiskey shop, and decided to jump into the lake. On the way, he passed the mission. As he listened to the old Gospel songs, he involuntarily stopped. He was dirty, not having washed for days; he wore an old pair of trousers, a greasy old coat, no shirt and old shoes. Inside, he fell into a back chair by the wall. When the invitation was given, he shuffled front; tears had already cut two paths through the dirt on his face. He took Christ as Savior. The next day he walked all through the underworld district, stopping before each saloon and den with the prayer that God would give him strength never to go back again. He used to give his testimony night after night, saying: "God has kept me ever since."

The assistant superintendents during these years of transition served only short terms, though some of them did splendid yeoman's work. The longest term was served by Bob Ingersoll, acting superintendent from 1916 to 1918, who then went into wider evangelistic fields. It was during Ingersoll's time that Rob "Razer" Fenton, world-traveled pickpocket, was converted. Since then, Fenton has lectured around the states before service clubs and other groups on "Does Crime Pay?"

Another trophy for Christ was Buford K. Asper. It was on April 4, 1918, at ten minutes to nine, that all things became new for him, as he accepted Christ at the mission. An immediate desire to preach the Gospel moved him from the moment of his conversion. Nor was the Lord long in providing the opportunity. In the Dakota territory he served five small charges, not dismayed at the average of $18.43 for three months' material returns which the Lord provided for food, fuel, clothing and upkeep of the aged car that covered from 75 to 100 miles every Sunday in spreading the unsearchable riches in Christ Jesus.

The post-war civilization was one of moral disintegration and the mission's obligation was more tremendous and difficult than ever. Modernism had flooded the universities and many churches, and had now seeped through to the restless, dissatisfied army of street wanderers. Evangelists of national repute and rescue missions around the country were beginning to complain that it was harder to reach the masses.

Pacific Garden Mission trustees determined more than ever to hold the tiny lighthouse true to the Gospel. Colonel and Mrs. George R. Clarke, the founders, had been put to rest in Mount Greenwood Cemetery. The board was enlarged from twelve to fifteen trustees, and A. M. Johnson, the president, requested that a creed be drawn, based on the Scriptures and similar to that used by Moody church to which board members should subscribe. It required belief in the inspiration and supreme authority of the Scriptures; the deity of our Lord Jesus Christ, His incarnation, atoning death, bodily resurrection and personal return; the Holy Spirit and His work essential to the regeneration and the sanctification of believers; the church of Christ on earth composed of the redeemed who are commissioned to make their chief business the evangelization of the world. Positive evidence of the departure from the fundamental doctrines was to be cause for the severance of relations with the mission.

But the mission leaders did not lose themselves in framing creeds, for their main emphasis was to reach the lost. When the influenza epidemic swept Chicago in post-war days, work continued in the spirit of Mother Clarke's ministry. The mission had never missed a night, but the city authorities insisted that the meetings be cancelled as a health measure. The mission was determined to keep the lighthouse aglow. The workers promised to leave the windows and doors wide open during the meeting, and finally the city consented. That first night proved one of the coldest of the whole winter; the thermometer hovered near zero, and the mission circle shivered in its overcoats. But there was a good crowd, and the testimonies sounded a bit more glorious than ever. "If they can keep Hinky Dink's open, and send folks to hell," said one convert, "I guess we can keep the mission open, and help folks get to heaven."

## Chapter XI

# A TWENTIETH-CENTURY JONAH

The old Van Buren street mission had two doors. For several years Mel Trotter took one and Walter Taylor the other, distributing tracts and inviting passersby to come in.

Trotter and Taylor were both babes in Christ. Mel learned that Taylor was studying at Moody Bible Institute, so, when the crowd at the door lessened, Mel turned and said: "What's your opinion of the seventh chapter of Romans?"

"The seventh of Romans—," answered Taylor. "Frankly, I've never read it."

Twenty years later, when Mel needed a man to shepherd Pacific Garden Mission in the tradition of the Clarkes and Harry Monroe, he wired a firebrand named Walter Taylor. That night Taylor spent in prayer; he wondered whether the Lord or Mel was calling him. In the morning he answered: "Yes, I'll be there." That was the beginning of an eighteen year superintendency that was to add further miles of miracle to the record of the historic haven.

Walter Grand Taylor, one of eight children, was born October 19, 1865, in a bleak basement bedroom in Pittsburgh. He was forty percent Dutch and the rest real American, like many Pennsylvanians. His mother, a little red-haired woman, was a true Christian; his father, a tobacco manufacturer, had a deathbed repentance. As a lad Taylor sold papers and grew up with one of the toughest boys' gangs in the city. He even broke into freight cars, stole from wagons and fruit stands. He was never suspected of such misdemeanors and his marks were so good in high school that the faculty gave him a teachers' certificate. Only his youthful appearance prevented his securing a position as principal, so Taylor clerked for a contracting firm until he looked a bit older, and then became an assistant principal for a time. Then, deciding to work as stock clerk for a blast furnace enterprise, he plodded along at three dollars daily, working every day in the year. Next he became a traveling auditor, moving from New York to Minneapolis, Omaha and New Orleans. Then came the position as secretary-treasurer of a Chicago drug company, where he later was one of the three men entering into an eighteen-year agreement to take over the business.

The sudden death of Taylor's young wife brought deep sorrow into his life. She was a Christian and he knew she was ready to meet God. In memory he could not forget his past stubbornness at her entreaty, nor his complaints whenever she wanted to hold prayer meetings in their Ravenswood home. A dapper dresser, with wavy, golden hair and a heart set on making a fortune, Taylor had little use for religion. But now, instead of being the cocky, five-foot ten-inch, two hundred pound victor, he was a suppliant on his knees before God, a great burden upon his soul. He was converted that night, February 21, 1896, in his room, when he realized that his wife was already in heaven, but that he was lost.

Taylor had a great yearning to serve his new-found Lord, and prayed that he might be extricated from the long-term contract with his pharmaceutical partners. Not long after, the other partners bought his interest. Taylor went into Y. M. C. A. work, then attended Moody Bible Institute, where his practical work assignments carried him to Pacific Garden Mission. There he learned the art of soul-winning and met converts like Mel Trotter, Harry Monroe, and others, as well as Mother Clarke. His first convert was U. S. Abell, who came to the mission in 1897 and heard the testimonies. Taylor invited him to come to Jesus. Abell later became the well-known Gospel cartoonist.

In a Christian boarding house Taylor met "Bobbie," the young woman destined to become the mission's "Ma Taylor." At a song service, Taylor was asked to sing a baritone solo. When he asked for a volunteer pianist, Miss Ethelwyn Robinson responded. She was from the "Rockefeller Church" in Cleveland, dating her conversion in her home church, although she was spiritually kindled when she heard Dwight L. Moody in Chicago. They harmonized so well together that he sang into her heart and she played into his. When he found that she sang also, and that the Lord was willing, they were married by Dr. R. A. Torrey in 1898. Two years later Taylor was graduated from Moody Bible Institute. After a brief ministry in the Parkhurst Church House, New York, they went to Colorado for a year as home missionaries among the miners and railroad men. There, 8600 feet above sea level, Taylor felt convicted of sidestepping an earlier call to do mission work among down-and-outers.

He had not forgotten the call, yet how he had shuddered at the idea. Stunningly dressed, he used to do personal work in the mission, placing his arms around the shoulders of the outcasts as he dealt with them. Often Harry Monroe eased Taylor's arm from around the converts, but Taylor never questioned why. One night when Taylor was going home on the street car something bit him. He jumped violently. The same thing happened a second time. When Monroe told him that the cooties had taken a liking to him, Taylor felt convinced he wasn't called to mission work. It was the last time he got close enough to a prospect for heaven to encourage such relationships, at least, so Taylor thought. When the Lord spoke to him about rescue mission service, Taylor suggested that home missions would be an effective substitute.

The next week came a letter to Colorado from a mission superintendent in Montreal. "I heard you preach in New York City some time ago," he wrote. "I'm leaving my mission after ten years here, and feel you and Mrs. Taylor are God's choice to run it."

The Taylors reached Montreal with five dollars in their pockets. On the way they stopped at Pacific Garden Mission for a moment with Harry Monroe, who knew something about the frigid religiosity of Montreal, and its lack of mission interest. "Taylor, you'll never stay there," he said, "it's such an ice house." Taylor nevertheless pressed on to Canada, started raising spiritual energy and a mustache. For sixteen years he and his wife carried on in the Old Brewery Mission, so named because it had its beginnings in an abandoned brewery. There were hundreds of converts—doctors, lawyers, businessmen, as well as immigrants and the downtrodden. During their ministry, the Taylors started the first Gospel fresh air camp among rescue missions, sponsoring a free two-week summer holiday, with the objective of preaching the Gospel to folks away from home. In two months they reached 2500 women and children, and despite a successful city mission work, won more souls in the fresh air camp than in the converted brewery. That gave them a great vision for mass evangelization, but they could not find among mission supporters financial help consonant with their desired outreach, so they resigned in 1916.

Mel Trotter had just asked Bob Ingersoll to become assistant at Pacific Garden Mission. When he heard that the Taylors were looking for a field with promise, he asked them to step into Ingersoll's mission in Columbus, Ohio. They plunged into the new soul-saving work with vigor. From there, Taylor went into the chaplaincy under the Y. M. C. A. in Alabama, serving for six months as director of religious work at Camp Sheridan.

Then, in 1918, another telegram came from Mel Trotter. The old Chicago lighthouse needed a keeper. Ingersoll felt his work as assistant superintendent was finished and Trotter felt that the other demands upon his own time were too great for his continuance as general superintendent. Mother Clarke had left the mission, not in writing but by preference, to Mel, and he felt that the hour had now come for the Taylors to take over.

Taylor arrived September 3, 1918, and Mrs. Taylor came September 15. They were destined to stay for eighteen years, during which time the mission was to sustain its reputation, already world-wide, as a great soul-saving station.

As Taylor walked in through the mission doors, he remembered how Mel Trotter used to stand with him night after night. Then he chuckled. "Yes, Mel," he thought. "I've read the seventh of Romans—and the eighth chapter too!"

## Chapter XII

## FIVE FEET FIVE INCHES OF SNOW

For a quarter century George Delos Snow made a living by gambling—cards, dice, horses. One night the side street gambling house in which he held a fourth interest netted $1150 profit in the first three sittings. Snow dealt cards like a Thurston. Only a handful of unsuspecting people and an hour's time were necessary for a killing.

In 1873, the year many Kansans went bankrupt, Snow was born in Garnet, Kansas, in the middle of a family of five children. His father was a grain dealer; his mother a praying Christian. Snow thought he could startle the world with a seventh-grade education, so went to work for a school supply house and then became a bank messenger in Chicago.

Soon he fell in with a card-playing crowd. He didn't know the first thing about poker, except that it was a costly game. Losses of ten and fifteen dollars a night were quite a bit for a young fellow like him, so when Snow's mother bought a house in another part of the city it wasn't difficult to accept lodging with her. Sometimes the urge came to see the gang, and he took the four-mile street car ride to renew acquaintances.

One day one of the old circle, an insurance salesman, confided that he had half interest in a gambling house at California and Madison, and offered Snow a job there.

"I don't know anything about gambling," he retorted. "Why do you want me there?"

"You don't have to know much. You can open up in the morning and sell cigars over the counter, can't you? And if a crap game starts, just take a nickel off each lick for being gamekeeper. And if they play pitch, take a dime off each lick."

When Snow thought about the thing, he decided it wasn't so bad. Fair salary, meal ticket at a nearby restaurant, and off for home at night by six o'clock so he wouldn't have to stay for the poker games after dark—not bad, he thought. He was twenty-three years of age at the time. He never told his mother just what he did for a living.

For twenty-five years thereafter Snow made a living by getting other people's money.

He stayed with the first job five years and started to go down from the first step. In this cigar store, where the three rooms were divided for smokers, pool players, and the card and dice sharks, Snow mixed in the card games. Soon he became a shill, who is to a gambling house what a decoy is to wild ducks. When the card game gets underway, a shill sits in the game, secretly playing for the house; when a live customer walks in, that is, a customer with money, the manager taps the shill on the shoulder or gives him a less conspicuous signal, and the shill steps out. Sometimes there are two and three shills in a game; if one shill goes, another quite likely wins, but in any event, the house always gets the ante of ten or fifteen cents a hand, or a quarter a hand if the stakes are big.

The den for which Snow worked wasn't making enough money, so the manager hired a professional cheater. Good-looking, well-dressed and slick, he was a high-class bottom dealer; that is, he dealt cards from the bottom as well as the top of the deck, so that it almost took a magician to tell the difference. A clever bottom dealer could be surpassed only by an expert second dealer, one who could deal from below the top card without detection. The shills could spot a bottom dealer because he held the deck unnaturally; they could tell a second dealer by a peculiar swish of the cards when he dealt a hand. That is why gamblers like music.

Snow usually sat to the right of the cheater, who knew how to give the live customers just enough leeway to make them reckless. Then he used his tricks to the advantage of the house. He would deal the hands, five cards to a player before bets were made. Bids would soar. Then the cheater used any of a dozen methods—palming, deck cutting by a slight crimp when the cards were passed to Snow, bottom or second card dealing, and signals. Not only were the cards marked on the back for easy identification, but the cheater wore a ring with a tiny mirror. Years later Snow met the cheater quite accidentally. The card shuffler confided that he had forsaken bottom dealing and was now one of the best second dealers in the world.

From that job Snow went quickly to the gambling houses. For a number of years, like any live customer, he played for himself against the rest of the group and the house cheater. Drinking took him for two or three years, but Snow found that he couldn't play good cards under the influence of liquor. But it wasn't easy to make a living playing free lance. The houses had watchers of their own; they were bent on making money, and wanted no cheater but their own to take the pool. Sometimes Snow was on the verge of a big take, but didn't dare bottom deal, for fear the shills would detect him, so took the loss. Sometimes he had courage enough for a shady maneuver and won.

One day a card player came to him and said, "I want you to cheat a friend of mine tonight. We can take him at poker, and we'll split, half and half." It was two in the morning when they reached the friend, a saloonkeeper who was just closing for the night. They played until dawn. Then the right moment came. The saloonkeeper had a great hand and bet heavily. Snow dealt, slipping himself a card from the bottom of the deck. The saloonkeeper lost $260 that night. Snow lent him enough money to open business in the morning.

By this time Snow no longer lived with his mother, but he made it a point to visit her for a day every few months. She never dreamed he was a gambler, and talked to him about the Lord. One evening when she asked him to go with her to Pacific Garden Mission he rebelled. "Why did I ever come out here today?" he asked. "Am I that bad?" But she wouldn't be refused. Not wishing to displease her, because he saw her so few times and was more or less the family black sheep, Snow and his gray-haired mother of seventy took the street car to the mission. He sat with her a few rows from the rear. He was quite disinterested. After the service when Mrs. Clarke came and asked him "Are you saved?" he muttered "Yes," in an aside that his mother could not hear. Then they left. Snow continued gambling for thirteen years.

Only one thing kept George Snow from opening a gambling house of his own: fear that his mother would discover the truth. It was an easy way to make a small fortune, while others, the cheaters and shills, would be doing the actual nasty work and the house enjoyed half the stakes. For two years he tried to break from gambling, and got a job on the outside. Every free day, however, found him gambling again, and winning meant cheating. Hadn't he lost $125 in a few games with the old timers by playing the cards straight? And he couldn't break the slump.

The gamblers liked him. Many houses wanted a good cheater, and Snow had many offers. He made ten or fifteen dollars a night for himself, while a hundred or a hundred fifty went to the manager, so he went back to the dens. He fell in with bad women. Then came the tobacco habit that finally meant an operation for cigarette cancer.

One night in the old gambling house he determined to quit. They had played a new game—stush, they called it—and he couldn't win. He didn't know it well enough to cheat. Anyway, he was tired of cheating and his heart felt as black as ink. His health was broken and he had only six months to live. He determined to return to the old mission to be saved.

"Then the devil got after me," said Snow. "The devil said, 'Would you have the crust to go down to a church or a mission after the life you've lived?' That was the way he talked me out of it. A few nights later I decided I'd go anyway. Then the devil said, 'Do you think it's fair to give Jesus the worst part of your life?' So I didn't go that night either. The next time I wanted to go, the devil said, 'What will the gang say?' Well, I knew the gang all right; they'd think I was crazy. But I was sure, too, that if I had a few thousand dollars on me, they'd probably kill me to get it. Then the devil began listing my sins. He kept it up for three hours—listing one sin right after the other. When he finished, I said, 'That's right; I'm a sinner, and you haven't missed a one. My heart is black.'"

The next night Snow walked out of the gambling house on the north side of Madison street. As soon as it was dark, he boarded a street car for the mission. He hoped it would be open. It was a cold February night and he had only $2.50— and borrowed money at that—in his pocket. Finding his way to 67 West Van Buren street he went to the door. It opened, but inside everything was dark. He looked at his watch. It was only seven. He decided he was early, so he walked the street for a while and then waited under the elevated pillars. He hoped there would be a meeting, for he wanted desperately to be saved. Suddenly a few people appeared and walked into the mission room. He followed and sat down. Folks kept coming. Walter Taylor, the superintendent, wasn't there that night because it was his free night, but Snow didn't know the difference. An evangelist got up and spoke. Snow kept **hoping he would stop and that there'd be an altar call. Then** a mission man took the platform and called for testimonies. Snow learned later he was T. B. Davis, now a Detroit pastor. "Lucky" Baldwin was among the witnesses that night. Snow kept hoping more and more that an invitation would be given. Finally Davis closed the testimony period and said, "Is there a man who wants to be prayed for tonight?" Snow sat still. Someone raised a hand; then another hand went up. Snow followed. "Will you go a step further? Those who raised your hands, come to the front for prayer," added Davis. Snow went up and took the last place on the left side of the platform. He kept wishing that he were saved. Davis began on the other end of the platform, whispering to each penitent, but Snow couldn't understand a word. Finally he came to Snow and asked, "Are you a sinner?" Snow said, "Yes." "If you asked Jesus, do you think he'd forgive you?" questioned Davis. "I do," said Snow. Then they prayed together the publican's prayer, "God be merciful to me, the sinner."

Snow went back to the meeting the next night. He enjoyed every minute of it, never dreaming he might be asked for a testimony. When the time came, Walter Taylor called for witnesses. "I almost fell out of the chair when the thought gripped me that I would be expected to say something. Then the devil said to me, 'Don't *you* get up.' I started up three times but slid back. Then Mr. Taylor said, 'Somebody will lose his testimony if he doesn't get up.' With that spur, I sprang to my feet and whipped out the words, 'I was in here last night. I used to gamble for a living but Jesus saved me.' Then I dropped into my chair. Taylor shouted to the crowd, 'Let's give him a hallelujah.' They shook the house with that cheer; I can still hear the place ring."

That was February 11, 1919. A quarter of a century a gambler and a quarter of a century a Christian layman is George Snow's story, for next February will be his twenty-fourth spiritual birthday. He has used the intervening years to God's glory, testifying in churches, missions and on street corners. Whenever he can, he still makes his way to the noon street meeting conducted by the mission at State and Harrison, and, with some tickets for a religious rally demonstrates some of the tricks by which he cheated men before Christ saved him. He weighs one hundred ninety pounds, has light blue eyes set in a round, ruddy face, and white hair. He usually begins his testimony by saying, "Well, here stands five feet five inches of Snow." He has worked as a silk salesman and dry goods clerk, proclaiming the good tidings to many hungry souls. He gives a dollar a week to foreign missions alone.

When Snow was saved three months, the superintendent, Walter Taylor, asked for volunteers for a street meeting. Snow had another spiritual struggle. "The devil said, 'If you go, I'll have the gang out from the west side to hear you.' The more I resisted, the more guilty I felt. Finally I wanted to run out of the mission. But then Mr. Taylor walked by, and I said, 'I'll volunteer to give my testimony at the street meeting.' Taylor smiled and said, 'I knew you would.'"

When Snow found out that the meeting would be held at Quincy and State streets the news almost unnerved him. He had still another struggle. The reason was quite evident. When he gave his testimony, he said, "Right up there, on the fourth floor of that building, is a gambling hall. Swell chance you had when you walked in there. There were eight of us who worked as shills for the house. We would hang around and read the papers until the elevator bell rang. Then we would dive for the table, cards and chips. We made believe it was a terrific game with tremendous stakes. Then, after three or four rounds, one of the shills would say, 'Cash me in. I've got a date.' Invariably one of the newcomers stepped into the game. He hardly had a chance, with five shills and a couple cheaters against him. Why, we'd clean him right out. These cheaters knew some tricks that I never could explain, and I used to be a cheater myself. But then Jesus saved me. He saved me at the Pacific Garden Mission, just the other night."

## Chapter XIII

## PORT OF MISSING MEN

More than ever, under the regime of "Dad" and "Ma" Taylor the humble mission was to become a temporary drydock for missing men—absent for long years from their homes and families, and absent for a night from their gambling and drinking hovels. Some of humanity's hopeless hulks were to tug themselves into the port for help, leaving with new power and a new Captain.

There was a great inheritance of converts, eager to tell the story and to help Taylor send forth the light to the ends of the city. Among them was Honey Briscoe, a colored octogenarian who had a great testimony. His real name was Christopher Columbus Briscoe. While in politics, he acquired an appetite for drink that in ten years made him a physical wreck. When Mayor Swift closed the city's gambling houses, the establishment at State near Polk where Briscoe stayed was padlocked and he was put out on the street. From his first sleeping place, a barrel house at Polk and Clark streets, he trickled into the hobo lines and slept in the box cars that fringed State street between Polk and Twelfth streets. One night while sleeping under an old building he was disturbed by music and singing. Another sleeper said it was the Pacific Garden Mission folks. Briscoe rolled out. There on the street corner he saw about a hundred men of his own class listening to a group of witnesses. After the service everyone was invited to come to the mission. Briscoe slipped into the hall with the rest of the crowd. He had never heard singing or testimonies like this before. Several nights afterwards he returned to the mission, yet always saying to himself, "This certainly can't be for me; I must die a drunkard." One night Mother Clarke saw him raise his hand. Coming down from the platform, she led him to the front, and there he took Christ as Savior. For the first time in ten years he tasted no liquor the next day. He came to the mission faithfully from the time of his spiritual birthday in 1895. When he reached eighty-five years of age, he was called the "Dean of the Mission," for he was its oldest convert. They also dubbed him "Honey" Briscoe because he called so frequently for that chorus, "There's honey in the

rock for me." He could pray until the very heavens opened;
the young converts said it was because he had been at it so long,
but others knew that he stayed near to Christ. He gave his
testimony in power, and when he finished with the words, "It's
most time for me to be goin' home with the Lord, 'stead of
stayin' 'round down here," the Taylors thanked God for the
great stream of converts such as Briscoe, who told redemption's
story, and prayed God's further harvest of souls.

From the very start that prayer was answered. Scores of converts were made with the passing months, many of whom went
into Christian service. Their testimonies fascinated the newcomers to the mission and often proved the opening wedge for
the Gospel.

An elderly Swede, just turned sixty-five, made up his mind to
take his life in Lake Michigan. It was a disagreeable, gloomy
Sunday, January 26, 1919; the streets, covered with slush, were
almost empty. Reared in a fine Christian home by a devout
mother, well-educated, and with every reason for a bright
prospect, he lost all his friends by dissipation and wanted now to
forget. Just as he braced himself for the plunge, a policeman
approached. The Swede walked aimlessly to the Northwestern
Railroad station and there destroyed every article that might
identify him as G. A. Lind, once a successful furniture finisher
and polisher. Then he went again to the lake, but again somebody was nearby. He waited until after dark, walking nervously
up and down the loop streets to pass the time. At one place he
heard music and singing and saw a big electric sign with the
words, JESUS SAVES. Poorly dressed men went in, he noticed;
finally he followed, too. Hearing testimonies by ex-gamblers,
ex-drunkards, ex-convicts, he knew these people had found a
great power. When the invitation was given, he burst into tears
and went forward. With his new-found Lord he went from
city to city, preaching the Gospel on faith, and winning many
converts. He called himself "God's little errand boy," and told
over and over how during his dissipation he tried to prove to
himself the non-existence of God and of a hereafter, but how
Christ became real in his life and broke the shackles of sin.

Nor was the mission a haven for men only. Needy women
also found Christ at its altar, and came back to tell the story
There was Hattie Matthews, who drank so heavily that one Sunday night she looked at the bottle in her room and said, "I'll die
rather than take another drink." She was such a victim of

liquor that the thought of death seemed sweet to her. She had
spent most of her life with "the gang" in a State street theatre,
when she wasn't working in a Lake street restaurant. After the
Sunday show the crowd had said, "Good-bye, we'll see you tomorrow." But Hattie's mind was made up; there would be no
tomorrow. She boarded an eastbound Van Buren street car to
the end of the line, but by mistake alighted at the wrong corner.
Looking up she saw in big red letters, JESUS SAVES. She walked
right into Pacific Garden Mission and marched to the front row.
"I thought all the sinners always sat in the back, so I would fool
everybody." she said. She felt tortured throughout the service;
a dozen times she wanted to run out to the lake, but a man with
a crutch was sitting next to her and she could not get out. The
music, singing and testimonies made her hard and rebellious.
During the invitation a chorus was sung:

> "They crucified Him, they crucified Him,
> And nailed Him to a tree.
> And there He died, a King crucified,
> To save a poor sinner like me."

That melted Hattie's heart, and she cried out for Jesus to save
her. Superintendent Taylor noticed her in the crowd, and asked
the congregation to repeat the chorus. Hattie didn't come forward, but Taylor realized later that the crutches were in the way.
After the meeting she knelt at the altar and gave her heart to
Christ. In another state Hattie took the good tidings to her
mother, who two years later died a Christian with a Christian
daughter at her side.

Joe Lightfoot wrestled for half a century with King Alcohol.
He took his first drink when he was seventeen, and he was not
yet twenty-one when he had delirium tremens. Soon crazed by
drink, he took pledges, oaths, and every remedy he heard of; he
took the "gold cure" twice. His godly mother prayed for him
and pleaded with him. On her deathbed she held Lightfoot's
hand and begged him to take Christ as Savior. He had been
drinking, and would not kiss her in that dying hour because of
the smell of liquor on his breath. When she died, Lightfoot
went out and got drunk. Downhearted and discouraged, his mind
blackened by the thought that he was doomed to a drunkard's
grave, he wandered on a March night in 1919 into the mission.
A man named Holland Oates was speaking on how God delivered
him from the curse of John Barleycorn. A ripple of hope thrilled
Lightfoot's heart. He went forward and was saved. **Night**

after night he told drunkards that there was but one cure—not an oath, not a pledge, not the "gold cure," but only the "blood cure."

Stranger than fiction reads the story of Elmer Wagler, whose speech impediment carried him to a Chicago school for stutterers, from where he went with some improvement to small office jobs. Rooming at the Y. M. C. A. hotel, he wandered occasionally to the mission, where, on February 27, 1921, he received Christ. He had a burning desire to testify, but every time he arose to his feet, he stammered so much it was pathetic. He would turn fiery red and blurt, "Jesus saved me." Walter Taylor took hold of him one night after the meeting and told him to get his mind away from his impediment. "When you give your testimony," Taylor said, "put out your left hand and bang your right fist against the back of the chair—anything to take your mind off your throat!" After that Wagler discovered that he had unusual freedom when giving his testimony. A few weeks later he told his story in a street meeting, and, in the power of a new life, became head of the Southern Highland Evangel with its Gospel Ministry in "the land of do without."

The following month the stream of converts included a colorful chap named George Quilty, an electrician. As a youth he had learned his catechism, but thought that anyone who wasn't a Jew was a Christian. Later he took Christ as Savior, but never learned the meaning of a consecrated life. Quilty spent his time around the engine house of a Chicago fire department company, where a worker preached to him now and then. One night he spoke about the second coming of Christ and got Quilty a Bible. They went up in a hay loft to read. Looking down, they saw the men playing pool and betting on the horses in an adjacent room. "Don't pray for them," said the worker, "because it won't work." Then he invited Quilty to a mission service. They went to Pacific Garden Mission on Saturday night, March 12, 1921, and Quilty raised his hand during the invitation. Back among his co-workers, Quilty preached the Gospel to them. He helped hold meetings in front of his place of employment where there were 30,000 workers, did jail visitation on Sundays, and testified from street corners and church pulpits.

Louis Skoda was baptized a Roman Catholic on Chicago's west side. The pictures of the saints in his mother's German Catholic testament were his only knowledge of the Bible. Skoda wandered into the mission July 9, 1921, a warm night, raised his hand for prayer, and was saved. He parted company with the clubs in which he was a familiar figure, and with the west side's Valley Gang. Except for his father, he led the home circle of nine to Christ, told his story wherever he went, then started a south Chicago mission.

It wasn't all sunshine for the mission converts after conversion. Some of them held on to old sins for a time, and faced great spiritual struggle, but Walter Taylor did his part to bring them to full surrender. Such a struggle came into the life of A. A. Bedell, the Michigan Central brakeman. At sixteen his parents took him from school because of an incurable nervous trouble resulting from overstudy; specialists had pronounced his case as hopeless. He went to work for the railroad, but suffered physically for twenty years. Several times he passed the mission and wanted to go inside, but lacked the courage. On Sunday, November 21, 1921, however, he stepped inside the door. Mrs. Taylor led him to a chair. Although he made a profession of faith, he backslid six months later. Then came full consecration to the Lord, and with his wife, the beginning of a godly home. He told his story so compellingly in his home church that at the mid-week prayer meeting they still pray for Pacific Garden Mission.

The last Saturday night convert in the old mission at 67 West Van Buren street, before its removal to the present location was Jake Zimmerman, who showed his gratitude for the Gospel message by tending the mission door at its new site for years after his conversion. Zimmerman was born in Hungary, left home at eighteen, and became a waiter in half the roll call of the United States. His chief sin was gambling. Coming to Chicago in 1910, he attended the mission off and on for thirteen years. He probably turned down the Gospel invitation more times than any other man at the mission. He was invited about a thousand times to accept Christ, including some fifty invitations by Mother Clarke. Yet he kept refusing. Then he wandered into the Van Buren street refuge on its last Saturday night, January 27, 1923, determined to yield to Christ. From the moment he went in, he found the call irresistible. There were other converts in the old mission the following three nights, but when it opened on Wednesday, January 31, for the noon-meeting at the new quarters on 650 South State street, it was Zimmerman who for six and one-half years became "a door keeper in the house of the Lord."

## Chapter XIV

## CALVARY COVERS IT ALL

More than passing interest centers in the stream of musical blessing that poured into the evangelistic world from the Pacific Garden Mission.

Quite symbolic were the visits to the shelter, in its first years, of Horatio G. Spafford, from whose burdened heart came that glorious gospel song,

> "When peace, like a river, attendeth my way,
> When sorrows like sea billows roll;
> Whatever my lot, Thou hast taught me to say,
> It is well, it is well with my soul."

He had written the words the year before Colonel and Mrs. Clarke began their mission on Clark street, after receiving a cable from Cardiff, Wales, in which his wife sent the message: "Saved alone." Their four children had perished in the Atlantic when the steamer Ville de Havre sank within a half hour after colliding with another vessel. Spafford spoke at the mission a number of times.

Music played an important part in the services and while the type was not reflective of the great cathedrals, yet it was conducive to a spiritual work in the hearts of drunkards, gamblers and outcasts. The old organ, still standing at the mission, provided a pleasant if wheezy contrast to the tinny instruments of the drinking dens, and its tunes were dedicated to God, as evidenced by the sign, "Ye must be born again," which was displayed near the manual in the days when Mel Trotter's brother, Bill, played the keys.

Through the years the mission inspired the writing of many Gospel choruses. One of the most popular was James P. Sullivan's "O Say But I'm Glad":

> "There is a song in my heart today,
> Something I never had;
> Jesus has taken my sins away,
> O say, but I'm glad!

"O say, but I'm glad, I'm glad,
O say, but I'm glad!
Jesus has come and my cup's overrun,
O say, but I'm glad!"

From a nearby tavern Sullivan had seen Harry Monroe come out of the mission. Attending the services a number of times, he never forgot Monroe's sweet voice as, with arms outstretched, he sang old Gospel hymns. Sullivan wished he had a relationship to God like Harry's, but for five years he went on in sin, until in 1912 he staggered from a Harvey, Illinois, saloon into a local mission and was converted. "Poor Harry's face always haunted one with his sweet singing," said Sullivan. "Now he has gone to heaven, but he never knew that his singing sank deep in a wild Irishman's heart. Some time ago his dear face came back to me. I seemed to hear him sing again, and I wrote the chorus, 'I Recommend Jesus to Thee,' which is having a reception something like my 'O Say, But I'm Glad.'"

Outstanding, too, among mission converts as a producer of Gospel songs was Scotty Lawrence. Talented as a songwriter, he once took a bet that in twenty minutes he could grind out a song that would sweep the country, and what's more, he made good on it. Then he fell into ribald theatrical company. Much in demand in social and theatrical circles because of his song hits, he soon fell victim to overpowering alcohol and drug habits. He drifted to Chicago, like many another human failure and outcast. In desperation, he stole openly in a large, Chicago department store, so the police would send him to the Bridewell for a six months sentence, which he thought might cure him. Upon his release he drifted back into the same old gang, none the better for his incarceration. Dozens of times he wandered into Pacific Garden Mission, prayed, professed Christ as Savior, and went out to backslide. He was perhaps the most prayed for man in America. In every mission in Chicago he had raised his hand for prayer, only to revert to drunken disgrace. It was a sorry state of penitence and drunkenness that made Lawrence despise himself. One night after professing Christ at Pacific Garden Mission, a trustee there bought Scotty a new suit of clothes. The very next day he appeared in overalls: he had been jackrolled and the suit taken from him. And he was drunk again. Finally one night in 1921, three godly women, Mrs. Taylor, Mrs. Wendell and Miss Hunter, a schoolteacher, knelt beside

him at the mission. One of them whispered, "Scotty, God
loves you." He gave his heart anew to God that night and
heard the very angels of heaven sing. The next song he wrote
was,

> "One day in sin I was told of a love,
> Coming from One who is reigning above,
> Gladly I listened, 'twas music to me,
> To know, though a sinner, that I could be free.
>
> *Chorus:*
> "Somebody whispered that Jesus loved me,
> Jesus who died upon Calvary's tree,
> Said He would save me, from sin set me free,
> Somebody whispered that Jesus loves me."

That song echoed from one mission hall to another as the
story of Scotty Lawrence was told, but the song-writer started
out on another search. It was for the girl who fourteen years
ago had promised to marry him if he came back sober, and a
Christian. He found her in New York, told her of Christ and
His power to save, and they had a joyful reunion. They spent
many successful years in the East in children's work. Meanwhile, too, Gospel song after Gospel song poured from Lawrence's heart, and Christians were carried nearer to God by
the noble words and music that flowed from his pen. "In the
Palace of God's Love" he dedicated to the Taylors.

> "Living for Jesus, dwelling in Him,
> Vict'ry is certain, no room for sin;
> Strengthened for battle, His presence near,
> Foes will be vanquished, no cause to fear.
>
> "Trials and temptations I take to Him,
> Because 'twas Jesus died for my sin;
> All day He's with me, 'tis Beulah land;
> He doth uphold me with His right hand.
>
> "Over in glory His face I'll see,
> Where there's a mansion waiting for me;
> How I adore my Savior, my King;
> That's why I love His praises to sing.
>
> *Chorus:*
> "I'm dwelling in the palace,
> In the palace of God's love;
> Each day brings a message
> From heaven above,
> Whispering so sweetly,
> He loves even me;
> I'm dwelling in the palace,
> In the palace of God's love."

When he died, his widow wrote to Pacific Garden Mission: "He more than made good and all who knew him loved and respected him. He was a ray of sunshine and our love was a beautiful, sweet and perfect love. My memories are a sermon in themselves, and I know Scotty is near me always. He couldn't help but be, he loved me so dearly. I held his hand as he crossed over and he knew me and kissed me, and I said, 'Everyone loves you, dear. Jesus loves you and everything is all right.' He smiled, said, 'Yes,' and in a few minutes was with his Master. His passing was as sweet and quiet as a baby falling asleep."

The song, "Show Others What Jesus Can Do," for which Scott Lawrence wrote both words and music, as is the case with all the other selections quoted in these pages, is a beautiful testimonial to God's working in his life:

> "Prove by the smile on your face ev'ry day,
> Prove by the wisdom He gives when you pray,
> Prove to the world there is no other way,
> Show others what Jesus can do.

> "Prove by the burden you're willing to bear,
> Prove by the comfort and cheer which you share,
> Prove in His service you'll go anywhere,
> Show others what Jesus can do.

> "Prove by each act you're a child of the King,
> Prove that you fear neither life nor death's sting,
> Prove by your faith till in Glory you sing,
> Show others what Jesus can do.

*Chorus:*

> "Show others what Jesus can do,
> Show others what Jesus can do;
> Through His grace from above,
> Give the message of love, and
> Show others what Jesus can do."

Scott's song, "Whisper a Prayer," was sung at the funeral service:

> "Whisper a prayer in the morning,
> Just at the break of the day;
> Why fear the fight, in your battle for right,
> When you know He will lead all the way?

> "Whisper a prayer at the noon-time,
> Pause in the midst of the throng,
> Look unto Him, Who can conquer all sin;
> In thy weakness, in Him thou art strong.

"Whisper a prayer at the twilight,
After the day's work is done,
No other friend will prove true to the end,
Like Christ Jesus, the Crucified One.

*Chorus:*

"Whisper a prayer,
Just whisper a prayer,
Even a whisper He'll hear over there;
Vict'ry is thine,
In love so sublime,
When to Jesus you whisper a prayer."

But it was the mission's own Ma Taylor who, probably more than any other, sent a deluge of inspiring choruses to the evangelistic world. Almost sixty Gospel songs flowed from her pen from the day that Dr. Towner paid her five dollars for "Jesus Only" and introduced it in his Moody Bible Institute song book. For sixteen years at the mission Ma Taylor played the piano and organ with an increasing awareness of the place of Gospel music in the ministry.

Her most popular number, "Calvary Covers It All," she wrote at the mission. The chorus came to her on the platform at 650 South State street when Charles E. Crawford, then with the American Bible Society, was giving his testimony. Crawford told how, when he entered full-time Christian service, his district manager handed him an application issued by a bonding company, since all employees of the organization served under bond. "My heart sank," said Crawford, "for I knew that in the light of my record before conversion no bonding company would accept the risk." When he told the manager his story, the superior officer said he was sorry, but he was powerless in view of a century-old rule that all employees must be bonded, and that Crawford would have to seek another position. Broken in heart, Crawford stole away to the shipping room to find relief in prayer. The manager came upon him unexpectedly, expressed his regret, but said the company would give him adequate time to secure another job. The following week the district manager summoned him and said that the governing board had unanimously agreed "that in spite of the fact that my record was black as midnight before conversion, since that now Calvary covers it all, I was to continue my work serving without bond and with an increase in salary."

For two decades Crawford served the firm becoming district sales manager for eleven states. Out of his testimony that night came Ma Taylor's

> "Calvary covers it all,
> My past with its sin and stain;
> My guilt and despair
> Jesus took on Him there,
> And Calvary covers it all."

Ma Taylor showed the complete song to Homer Hammontree who introduced it at the Church of the Open Door, Los Angeles, where four thousand sang the words. From there it spread through California and around the country. Robert Harkness, Harry O. Anderson and Harry Ironside began using it during campaigns. Then it was sung in England, Scotland, India and China, and J. Edwin Orr used it in his successful soul-winning campaigns in South Africa.

Among Ma Taylor's other well-known compositions is "Kept in Christ, I'm Satisfied," which Walter MacDonald uses extensively today, as well as her "As Far As the East." The former number was written under the drive of mission work, and dedicated to Pa Taylor during his superintendency:

> "Satisfied my soul's deep longing,
> When in Christ my soul doth hide,
> When the snares my footsteps thronging,
> I have Him, there's naught beside;
> Satisfied, O precious knowledge,
> Kept in Christ, I'm satisfied.

> "Kept in Christ, I'm satisfied,
> When in Him my soul doth hide;
> Ev'ry need by Him supplied,
> Kept in Christ I'm satisfied."

MacDonald, probably the outstanding mission convert in Taylor's regime at 650 South State street, fell asleep one night while visiting at the home of Christian friends. He had been in the midst of a pressing program of evangelistic meetings. Suddenly, in his sleep, he began to sing. The words were among his favorites, and none other than this song.

Among the most recent Gospel choruses inspired through Pacific Garden Mission's soul-saving ministry is that entitled, "Have You Heard the News?" composed by Herbert Claar, once mission pianist. It was at 650 South State street that on August 14, 1940, Claar found Jesus Christ the Savior from sin, and the All-Sufficient One. That is why he could write:

"Have you heard?  Oh have you heard the news?
Salvation is a gift to you and me,
Don't delay, Receive the gift today,
Jesus paid it all on Calv'ry's tree, Hallelujah!
Praise the Lord, King of glory,
Him crucified, it's the new old story,
He'll fulfill, For whosoever will
Shall be saved!  Saved!  Saved!"

For a number of years Dad and Ma Taylor's secretary and helper at the mission was Flora Rice, who had a beautiful soprano voice.  A promising college graduate, she looked to a vaudeville career while studying at Baylor University and Southern Methodist University, but when she was saved in her Texas church she wanted to enter Christian service.  For six and a half years she served the mission.  The night Hattie Matthews was converted it was Flora who sang the solo convicting Hattie's heart.  Later she married a Texas engineer, R. B. Alexander, who had been converted at the mission.

But the soul-saving station's musical contribution was only one of several functions secondary to its primary evangelistic purpose.  Many a young man entering the Gospel ministry won his first converts to Christ at the old lighthouse.  Among them was Dr. Joseph Croft Dent, retiring pastor of Chicago's Temple Baptist Church, who won his first soul for the Master when, as a student at Moody Bible Institute, he spoke at the mission.  Harry Monroe used to ask him to bring his concertina to lead singing in the Jackson Park meetings held for the men preparing the grounds for the Chicago World's Fair of 1893.

Many a servant of God, already trusting Christ for salvation, came into an experience of complete surrender at the mission.  Such is the story of John R. Rice, the "Will Rogers of the pulpit."  At the time he was a junior college teacher pursuing graduate work at the University of Chicago.  Rice was in the mission in May, 1921.  He saw sinners, almost hopeless in their despair, come to Christ and find inexplicable peace.  That night he promised God that "if He could help me save sinners He could have me to preach to sinners.  Thus I became a preacher of the Gospel of Christ."

Many a young convert learned his first lessons in pastoral theology at the mission.  Such was C. C. Beatty, later dean of Seattle's Northwest Bible Institute.  He came to Chicago with the World's Fair influx in 1893, and was saved at a mis-

sion service on Clark street conducted by Ed Card, a Pacific
Garden convert. Card brought him to Mother Clarke and
Harry Monroe. They put him to work taking the offering,
dealing with seekers at the altar, and giving his testimony.
One night Dr. R. A. Torrey, then president of Moody Bible
Institute, was to speak, but failed to appear. Monroe asked
Beatty at the last moment to give the evening's message,
making no explanation since half the audience did not know
Dr. Torrey was to come anyway. After that the mission boys
called him "Doc Torrey" in good-natured derision. After
serving a small church and several years of evangelistic work,
Beatty went into Bible Institute administration.

Many a sinner, outside of Christ, came into the mission only
to spurn his Savior's call. But by the scores they wrote in
later to tell that they found no peace until, at some meeting
elsewhere or alone in the closet of prayer, they made settled
accounts with the Master. Charles H. Miller was only one of
a whole family of them. He had spurned his mother's pleadings and sank into liquor and gambling. In a drunken stupor,
he felt the curse of delirium tremens coming upon him, and
wandered into what he thought was a long hallway. It
proved to be the mission room. John Wendell gave him a
Bible and the men knelt for prayer near the old organ. Miller
did not make a personal commitment, however, and things
became worse. Miller's mother held on in prayer. One night,
February 8, 1921, he staggered into another mission and was
saved. The next Saturday he testified at Pacific Garden Mission and went out to found the Beaumont Rescue Mission in
Beaumont, Texas.

## CHAPTER XV

## A BOX SEAT ON "MURDERER'S ROW"

One of the mission trustees sat successively on two Chicago street corners with an adding machine, tabulating the pedestrians. He was Louis A. Crittenton, general superintendent for a whole family of rescue centers to which Pacific Garden Mission had given rise. He was confirming the board's suspicion that "many more fish could be caught near State and Polk streets than at the Van Buren street location."

There was another factor in the desire for a new Pacific Garden Mission location. The rent at the old site was $5,500 a year. The lease was to expire May 1, 1922, and the owner wanted $12,000 to $14,000 a year for a five-year renewal. The trustees hesitated and named Crittenton a one-man committee to survey the loop for a new mission home.

Crittenton was in a good position to know the specific needs of the mission. As a boy in knee pants he started attending Colonel and Mrs. Clarke's mission ten years after its founding. He sang Saturday nights in the male quartet with Frank Webb, Chris Truelsen and Andy Blackstone, son of the author of "Jesus Is Coming." He spoke many times at Monroe's request. He was there the night Tom Mackey, the ex-prizefighter, was saved and saw him put up his hand for prayer, a strand of his torn overcoat hanging from his arm. Years later Crittenton was to become pastor of Chicago's Little Church on the Corner, where Harry Vom Bruch was converted under Mackey's preaching. He was at the mission the night Mackey was distributing tracts. A passerby spat on the convert. Mackey forgot himself, hit the man so hard that he went somersaulting into the gutter. In quick remorse Mackey ran to the curb and cried out, "Oh God, forgive me!" Mackey carried the man to the mission altar. When he regained consciousness, Mackey was praying over him. Crittenton was the trustee who bought Scott Lawrence a new suit back in the song writer's pre-Christian days, and talked with him about Jesus. From the Clarkes to the present day he knew the whole succession of superintendents.

Working with detectives against prostitutes and gamblers, Crittenton had given many nights to law enforcement. He won

111

394 cases out of 400, and his group of crusaders were the power that drove the red light houses after 1900 from behind the Van Buren street mission to Twenty-Second street. Later he confessed, however, that police seldom cured a lawbreaker. One night at a street meeting testimonies were given by Dick Lane, Tom Mackey and his wife, and others. Suddenly the door of a red light den opened. A half-naked girl ran into the street and rolled into Mrs. Mackey's long skirt. The madam of the house ran out, insisting that the girl be returned. Mrs. Mackey said, "This is my girl now—you go back, or you'll land in jail." That moment convinced Crittenton that there is no substitute for soul-reclamation outside of Christ.

Crittenton knew something about rescue mission objectives, too. When Dr. Harper, president of North Carolina's Elon College, came to Chicago in 1910 to buy a pipe organ, he wanted to see what the city was doing for its outcasts. Crittenton was then in the employ of the Kimball Piano Company. Part of his work was to show prospects the city. He was asked to fulfill Harper's request, which was not too difficult, since he delighted showing visitors the mission anyway. First he took Dr. Harper to the Art Museum and singled out a guard named Dick Ramey. "Meet President Harper of Elon College," said Crittenton. "He wants to know what Chicago is doing for its down-and-outers."

Tears came to Dick Ramey's eyes. He told how in 1857 he had been born on an Ohio river farm in southeast Indiana, and how he had begun spending his money in saloons the moment he started work on the steamboats plying the Ohio and the Mississippi. In 1889 Ramey's father was deathly sick and lay unconscious for several days. "One evening while alone with him," said Dick, "I thought that I could easily put my hand on his throat and finish the little remaining life there was in him. Suddenly the old man, who had battled adversity all his life, opened his eyes and looked at me as though he read my mind. O, such a look! Those eyes burned their way into my very soul. My brain was stupefied with whiskey, but I never forgot those eyes; I never smiled again until I knelt in Pacific Garden Mission on September 15, 1895." Then he told how, in May 1895, his wife died and was buried in a pauper's grave in Chicago. Ramey went back to his hovel of a home so drunk he did not remember how he got there. Four weeks later his little baby girl died. He had spent all he had on liquor, and, not having money enough for a funeral, buried her in a soapbox on the outskirts of his little home town. These incidents and the doctor's guarantee for him of only a short time to live, utterly destroyed any desire for life. He decided to end it all. Looking up into the blue sky he shouted, "The God that made me and made a hell to put me in, can put me there and be damned!" He went to Chicago. Walking north on Clark street Ramey saw the mission's Gospel wagon with a half dozen men who in a chorus repeated John 3:16. Then they sang a hymn, and Harry Monroe called on the men to testify. That night Ramey went to the mission. As he passed through the door he saw a small sticker with the words, "Get Right With God." By the old wall clock were printed the words of John 3:16; back of the rostrum, the phrase "God is Love" and "How Long Since You Wrote to Mother?" When Ramey heard that God is love, and that He had sent His Son to save even poor, ignorant and depraved wretches like himself, his stony heart was crushed. Tears of repentance and gratitude flowed that September 15, 1895. Two weeks later, Ramey went to the cemetery and arranged for the bodies of his wife and baby to be removed to a family lot. He went to work for the Art Institute for twenty years, and then returned to live on the farm.

The visiting college president could hardly restrain the tears as Ramey told his story. When he finished, Crittenton said, "Thank you, Ramey; we're going over to see Dick Lane now." There at the *Chicago Daily News* building, Lane, the exsafecracker, repeated the story elsewhere recounted in this book. Lane became a friend of Victor Lawson, publisher of the *News,* who had been converted under Moody's preaching and who left the mission $25,000 in his will. Dr. Harper was so impressed with the testimonies of the mission converts that he wrote an article on the mission for *Christian Century.*

Thus it was that many memories flooded Crittenton's mind as he kept count on his adding machine. He recalled how in 1920 the trustees had opened the Wilson Avenue Mission with Joe Meinardi and later Bob Ingersoll as superintendent; how in 1921 the trustees took over the State Street Mission and began another in the Woodlawn district with Warren Cole in charge. Crittenton was general superintendent of all these enterprises, but the most pressing task right now was to find a new home for "Mission Number One."

Billy Sunday, who had raised $70,000 in pledges for his spiritual birthplace during his Chicago campaign, and Mel

Trotter even more, recognized what reasons there were for a change. Sunday even wrote Mel that he would not object to using a part of his Chicago fund for the branch missions "if that seems the wisest thing to do in the furtherance of the work there in Chicago, but I would feel like depending upon your judgment in the matter. I suppose as the city grows, that conditions are naturally different than they were years ago." In fact, the matter of a new site had been discussed by the trustees with Ma Sunday and Mel Trotter back in 1918, before Sunday's ten-week campaign.

When Crittenton's tabulation showed that hobo paradise had shifted to such an extent that by a fair sampling the pedestrians on State street outnumbered those on Van Buren by seventeen to one, the trustees felt there was no alternative to moving. The directors held a spirited season of prayer in November, 1921, "for special guidance in connection with the crisis involved in finding a new home for the old Pacific Garden Mission." Trustees attending were George D. Elderkin, George D. Webb, Thomas S. Smith, Charles E. Coleman, John Timothy Stone, and general Superintendent Crittenton. The following March, two months before the Van Buren street lease expired, the trustees named a committee to negotiate a renewal for a year, so that no hasty action would be taken. There were several problems. Rumors were rife that, if Pacific Garden Mission moved to south State street, other parties were interested in beginning a mission at the old site. Further, the Van Buren property had fallen to a new lessee, a man named Myer, who offered to sublease to the mission; investigation showed, however, that he wanted $16,000 a year for a ten year period for the whole building. The trustees were interested in occupying only the first floor for another year.

Several new sites were possibilities. The old Park Theatre, now the State-Congress cinema, was rumored as available. A number of buildings in the six and seven hundred block on South State were for sale. Six months before May 1, 1923, the deadline on Van Buren, the trustees approached mission superintendent Walter Taylor for his views. He expressed readiness to abide by the board's decision, if they felt it was best to move.

The most promising site was a three-story brick building with a twenty-five by one hundred foot lot at 650 South State street. Meeting one day at the LaSalle street office of A. M. Johnson, head of the National Life Insurance Company, the entire mission board walked in a body to view the building. It was located on

"Murderer's Row," so named because more people were illegally killed on that street than on any other in Chicago. The building had sheltered the "White House," one of Chicago's most notorious and vicious dens. A veritable palace of sin, it occupied three floors and a basement. On the first floor was the long bar, reputed to be the longest in the world, and the hanging platform (the hooks from which it hung are still in the ceiling) where risque dancers and scantily clad entertainers held forth. So worn was the beautiful parquetry around the bar from endless shuffling that one of Dad Taylor's first tasks was to install a substantial flooring. The second floor was devoted to faro, roulette, and other games of chance. On the third floor were the painted ladies.

At the back was a hatchway, or trap door, which remains to this day. It was the reputed site of the historic Burr murder. Through it men were dumped like sacks of coal to the mud basement after being slugged or drugged and their pockets picked clean. Panderers, hanging near the Polk street station enticed victims to the joint. After being fleeced at cards, or stunned with knockout drops, the men were pushed through a door on the other side of which was a stairway. Unsuspectingly they stepped upon the trapdoor that worked at the press of a button, and were then hurtled helplessly to the mud-floored cellar. When reparations were made by the new owners, a reminder of prohibition days was found on the roof: several hundred pint and quart liquor bottles.

The street outside seemed like a suburb of hell. It was the main artery of the lodging-house district, where 5,000 men slept nightly. Flophouses and taverns were everywhere. Burlesque shows of the vilest kind played to crowds nightly. The labyrinth of lady barbers, pawn brokers, gambling dens, indicated man's extremity and God's opportunity.

The property owners asked $70,000 for the site. The trustees offered $60,000 cash but Max and Bertha Jesselson refused. Finally the committee bought it for $67,000 and the owners moved to California. Of that sum, two-thirds or $42,000 came from Billy Sunday's campaign. The balance came from Mother Clarke's estate. Crittenton took title to the property, then sold it to three trustees, who in turn transferred title to the mission, so that if any question ever arose, it would still revert to good hands. God's envoys had moved into the "White House."

CHAPTER XVI

RELICS OF THE PAST

No one dreamed of possible insurrection in the ranks when the decision was announced to move the mission to new quarters.

Some of the converts decided to stay at the Van Buren street site, which was a sacred Bethel to them. The ring-leader of the deserters was a converted drunkard, an old man, who told Crittenton to his face: "Do you see that plank right there on the platform? Twelve years ago my tears fell there when Jesus saved me. As long as I can say a word for my Savior, you'll find me carrying on by that spot for Jesus' sake. This mission has been a fixture at Van Buren and Federal streets for forty years!"

That was after the last scheduled meeting had been held on Van Buren street. For a moment Crittenton was stunned. Then he brightened. "Bully for you!" he answered. "That's the kind of stuff God needs on the firing line for souls. I want you to come out for lunch with me tomorrow."

Over the table the next day the converted drunkard repeated his whole story. "My testimony would never be the same," he said, "if I couldn't tell it down by the platform, right at the spot where Jesus washed my sins away."

Crittenton smiled broadly. "Then you'll have to move with us to 650 South State street," he said. "The carpenter has been working all morning. I asked him to take out a twelve-foot square of the platform and to move it to the new building."

The ex-drunkard, A. E. Nissen, put his head on the table and wept like a baby. Finally he shook hands with Crittenton and said, "I'm ashamed of myself, Crittenton. I'm just a miserable dog. If you'll forgive me, I'll stand right by the crowd on State street."

That chunk of platform wasn't the only relic that came from Van Buren street to the converted White House, nor was the twice-born drunkard the only convert. It was a wholesale moving day and when the mission opened on

Wednesday morning, January 31, 1923, for its noon meeting, it seemed just like home.

The previous night the *Chicago Evening Post*, in a spirited editorial, had wished the mission godspeed in its new location and anticipated the mingled emotions of those attending the last session at the historic Van Buren corner:

## THE PACIFIC GARDEN MISSION MOVES

Tonight there will be a gathering of the old-timers at 67 West Van Buren Street, where for forty years the Pacific Garden Mission has held open the door of hope and reached a hand of help to sin-burdened and broken men.

It will be the last meeting in the old hall. The mission is going to move. It is going to move nearer to those for whom it has prayed and labored. At 650 South State Street a three-story brick building has been secured, where another chapter in the long story of winning men back to self-respect and decency and usefulness will begin tomorrow night.

The Pacific Garden mission is a vital, throbbing part of the history of Chicago. It was founded by Col. and Mrs. George R. Clarke forty-five years ago. It was christened by Dwight L. Moody. For five years its work was carried on at 386 South Clark Street. From there it moved to the Van Buren Street building. The constituency it serves has shifted. South State Street is now the main artery of that lodging-house district which abounds in the flotsam and jetsam of life. Within a few blocks of its new quarters it is estimated 5,000 men sleep every night, men adrift on a stream of swift and precarious currents, homeless and friendless men, derelicts, "without God and without hope in the world." To breast that stream and rescue from it "whosoever will" is the mission's aim.

In tonight's meeting there will be many a human trophy glad to tell the story of how he was won by the word of sympathy, the strong and kindly hand of Christian comradeship, the message that God had a welcome and a place for him. And thoughts will turn to men who have carried the influence of the mission out into a wider field, and with lives redeemed from the waste heap have made an impress for lasting good upon their times.

Old-timers will recall Billy Sunday, whose first impulse to serve his fellows came in the Van Buren Street hall. Harry Monroe will be remembered with gratitude. He was converted in the mission and in 1892 became its superintendent. Then there was Dick Lane, expert in burglary, skilled user of "soup" when a safe stood in his way to "easy" money. Dick abandoned his profession when he heard the call to a better life. In his later years he numbered Melvin E. Stone and H. H. Kohlsaat among his intimate friends. Up in New York City Jack Callahan is devoting himself to the winning of men from its underworld. Jack was a pal of the notorious Butch Lyon, and a redoubtable west side gangster until he "found God" in the mission. Out in Japan, preaching the Gospel, is Bob Atchison. He is known internationally as a missionary today, but back in 1890 he was a Chicago slum derelict. Scores of business men's organizations thruout the country have heard "Razor" Fenton tell how, after winning notoriety as a pickpocket in Canada and the United States, he wandered into the Pacific Garden Mission and got a new vision and a new motive.

But the night will not be long enough to tell the whole story. Cartwright, oldest of living converts; Briscoe, Bob and Harold Oates, Snow, Mott, McCoy, and scores more will want to be heard. New names are being added to the list each week. Under Louis A. Crittenton, who once sold pianos, the work goes on. Chicago owes much to it. In the great maelstrom of the loop it has been lighthouse and life-saving station. We wish it godspeed in its new home.

In the new mission room Bill Hadley, Lew Speegle, George Snow, Razor Fenton, Honey Briscoe and other old-timers were as eager as ever to give their testimonies when Dad Taylor called for witnesses. And the crowds thronged to hear them. More than 5,000 men slept within a few blocks of the hall nightly and the unobtrusive salvaging corps, in the new slum district, found a new clientele. If Mel Trotter, after a surprise visit to the mission in its last months on Van Buren street, could report to the trustees that "great crowds are attending and many are being saved," so nonetheless Walter Taylor, by the time Crittenton had resigned his general superintendency in July, 1923, after maneuvering the shift to the White House, could report that "a great deal more was being done at the new location than at the old, and everybody was very pleased with the change in location." The mission's lifeboats were moving day and night among the human driftwood on State street and the record for remaking notorious safeblowers, pickpockets and other underworld characters was admirably sustained. Soon the mission was lodging between 250 and 300 men a night, the drifters finding a hardwood floor or concrete basement welcome change from the out-of-doors. Elderly men were sent to a cot in a nearby flophouse; boys under seventeen were sent to the Y. M. C. A. hotel. In the morning, everyone gathered for hot coffee and rolls. The only prerequisite for lodging and breakfast was attendance at the previous night's service.

Thus the mission carried on in the spirit of its founders. The wheezy old organ that Bill Trotter once played still bellowed the same hymns; the huge grand piano thundered out its praises to God. The cane-seated chair in which Mother Clarke used to sit, and the ponderous Bible which Walter Taylor once hurled at a dope fiend who pulled a gun on him, were all taken to the new quarters. The pictures of Colonel and Mrs. Clarke and the bronze plaques, the picture and memorial plaque of Monroe, were moved, too, as was the clumsy safe in which the mission funds were kept for years. The walls were decorated with Scripture quotations and pithy sermon thoughts. The painted messages included: CHRIST DIED FOR OUR SINS, HOW LONG HAS IT BEEN SINCE YOU WROTE TO MOTHER? BEHOLD NOW IS THE ACCEPTED TIME, BEHOLD NOW IS THE DAY OF SALVATION, CALL YE UPON THE LORD WHILE HE MAY BE FOUND, and others.

Behind the old walnut pulpit—a converted cabinetmaker had fashioned it for the Clarkes—Taylor put a small notice visible to the speaker. "Preach the Word 20 Minutes," it read, "Then People Will Not Sleep or Muse or Go Away." On the front, facing the audience, he placed a sign reading, "Jesus Never Fails." On top of the pulpit, peering over the edge of the big Bible, was the bronze plate reading, "Sir, We Would See Jesus!" One night when S. D. Gordon was guest speaker he changed his entire address after reading those words.

And from that old pulpit, through the years, great men and small, but Christians everyone, had proclaimed salvation's tidings. Dwight L. Moody on his infrequent visits was the first in a great succession. Mel Trotter, Billy Sunday, James M. Gray, R. A. Torrey, W. E. Biederwolf, William Evans, Paul, Luke and Lyell Rader, Harry Ironside, Herbert Lockyer, William L. Pettingill, Charles E. Fuller, William R. Newell, Anthony Zeoli, Peter W. Philpott, Paul W. Rood, John R. Rice, George Stevens, Harry Vom Bruch, William L. Ridgeway, Walter MacDonald, Peter Rees Joshua are only a few of the American "Who's Who in Evangelism" that have spoken from Pacific Garden pulpit in the course of the years.

The fire insurance underwriters had no spiritual sentiment when they valued the old organ at six dollars, the pulpit at one dollar, and the mission chairs at forty cents apiece. The mission converts preached a fire insurance of their own, and placed their own value on the treasures of the past, greatest of which was the good news that Jesus saves.

## CHAPTER XVII

# THE APOSTLE OF STATE STREET

The unabated influx of converts that marked the life-long history of Pacific Garden Mission was highlighted by colorful individuals all along the way. Dad and Ma Taylor's last thirteen years of service at 650 South State street, from 1923-1936, had their representative number, too.

It was a regular feature that Dumbbell Tilly and her group of girls, all of them in the early twenties, attended the mission once a week, no more, no less. They were a peculiar crowd, evidently given to the lures of drink and night life; nevertheless it would have been definite cause for alarm if Tilly, the apparent ring-leader, would not have made her weekly appearance with the group. Yet when Pa Taylor went to speak with her, the only response to his inquiry was a well-aimed punch in the stomach. For Miss Rice, the personal worker, there was not such violent reaction; quite on the contrary, absolute silence for over a month was the only answer she received. Then came the night of decision, when Flora Rice led Tilly to the Lord. And a leader of quite different calibre she proved to be. The mysterious Dumb-bell Tilly, it was discovered, was a cook on a large Evanston estate. Her pals were the other servants. Twelve friends, includ-ing the silver and kitchen girl, other cooks, and a sister, soon found the Lord through her new witness. She was strengthen-ing her spiritual muscles, hence the nickname which she still uses in correspondence with the Taylors. Tilly later married a Chris-tian man and named one of the children Flora, in honor of Miss Rice.

"They're all doin' it," was the excuse under which an Esthonian sailor justified his sin of drink and licentiousness. But when such a one leaves the sea to get rid of evil companions, it either indicates a weariness of life, or points to something better. For Otto Kiel it was both. He left the docks in New York in 1921 and came to Chicago, for many years not having written his Christian mother who since Kiel was three until the time he ran away surrounded him with Bible teaching and a godly life. Out of sheer curiosity he entered Pacific Garden Mission on May 14, 1923. The testimonies unearthed the long-dormant seed that his mother had planted in faith many years ago. At the invitation Kiel surrendered to Jesus, finding an immediate peace and joy that had never been his lot. It was a memorable letter of good news that reached a still-praying mother when Otto Kiel sent his testimony home.

Harry Venema, the native Dutchman, had a reputation, too— for profanity. This acquisition of questionable worth perhaps had an innocent beginning. Not knowing any English when he reached America's shores, he thought the language of his newly-found boisterous companions was of the best. Before long, Venema's vocabulary was his outstanding mark of identification It was miraculous how God cleansed him of this sin after September 7, 1924, the night Venema came to the Pacific Garden Mission and found Christ. All things, vocabulary included, truly became new. His vocation is that of a truck driver, an occupation he has used to spread his testimony throughout the miles of his business.

Royal L. Leeson thought sleeping in jails a real privilege. For a youngster exposed to his father's pool room lessons in smoking gambling and swearing, and branded with expulsion from school at the age of sixteen, the road offered many possibilities. There was a variety of short jobs from New York to Wyoming, from the Dakotas to Illinois, with the added fillip of a year in the army. A gambling house in Peoria, Illinois, took whatever cash he had, but an army officer of that town provided the necessary dollar for the stretch to Chicago. Working in a West Madison street restaurant two days produced four dollars, a state of unconscious drunkenness, and a rest at the Desplaines Street Police Station. The meal ticket which the Salvation Army Headquarters gave him to a Chinese shop on South State street brought him into Pacific Garden Mission territory. It was a rainy day, and he accepted the doorkeeper's invitation to the service. At least it meant getting out of the storm. Listening to the testimonies that rang out, Leeson was strangely affected. That day's plans, to obtain money by either robbery or holdup when night came, somehow lost their edge. He determined to get work and quit the old life. Unable to find work the next day, Leeson returned to the mission, stating his plight to the superintendent. Pa Taylor found work for him with a plumber, a Christian who gave him the money for the first meal in four days. That night, December 20, 1924, was the first time he ever knelt in prayer. Wanting to respond to the invitation at the mission, Leeson nevertheless hesitated doing so because of his ragged coat. Pa Taylor supplied his own, and in it Leeson fell to his knees and acknowledged his need of Christ and salvation. His testimony strengthened not only the witness of Pacific Garden Mission, but went with his missionary services into Central and South America.

Whiskey had such a hold on George Wells that he couldn't even attend to his unlawful business of bootlegging. And at home his two baby daughters were innocent victims of his vice, too. One Sunday morning, the memory of which now brings a shudder, found a doctor in the home. In a drunken stupor, Wells was just conscious enough to learn that he had poisoned the girls by giving them ginger-ale from the same glass he used for whiskey. God spared their lives for the later joy that came into a new Christian home when George Wells found Christ at Pacific Garden Mission. On January 25, 1925, while standing on State street waiting to pass some "stuff," Wells heard the singing from the mission. Walking into the hall, he heard the story of God's love for the first time in his life. He wept in repentance, and found freedom from sin in Christ Jesus. Immediately he secured new work, a position with the Volunteers of America which he holds to this day.

Louis Houge had been a backslider for many years. His two-thousand dollar pool-hall brought neither him nor the many patrons closer to God. Yet, night after night he visited Pacific Garden Mission. As he said in a testimony, "I kept coming to the Mission for many meetings. Mr. Taylor put his hand on my head one night as he urged me to let Jesus save me and said as I refused to go forward, 'My man, those gray hairs are not a good sign for your putting off the decision for eternity. You are too near the edge.' I didn't forget that." On September 2, 1926, he knelt at the mission in confession of sin, and arose to turn the key in his pool-hall for the last time. His work among railroaders is an excellent place for testimony, and he is active in jail visitation and in the work of the Christian Business Men's meetings.

In the summer of 1929, a college fellow with an automatic pistol in his pocket drifted into Chicago. Walking along on south State street, LaVerne Poole was attracted by the singing of a strangely familiar hymn, "What a Friend We Have in Jesus." He slipped out of Pacific Garden Mission as unobtrusively as he had slipped in. The next night, however, he was back again.

This time when the invitation to come to Jesus was given, a personal worker spoke to Poole about his relationship to Christ. He said he'd take a chance. Going to the altar, God's love so completely lifted him out of sin that LaVerne Poole's surrender was full and unreserved. Since that night, September 15, 1929, God's blessings have flowed in full measure. With a Christian wife, and strengthened for Christian service by seminary training, Poole is now working faithfully as a successful pastor.

Born in a parsonage, the son, grandson, and great-grandson of God-fearing clergymen, and himself preparing for the ministry, Otto P. Woysch nevertheless spent half a century in rank atheism. His was the best education obtainable. Leaving native Germany for Canada, he saw in the Northwest Provinces the opportunity for easy self-advancement. That was the reason for accepting a pastorate; he did not even believe in God, let alone believe in such a thing as God's call to His service. After a number of years of such hypocrisy, Woysch became an outstanding foreign language editor of several publications, all the while defying God, His church and work, in the most blatant manner. There came a day, however, when self-sufficiency vanished. Walking disconsolately into Pacific Garden Mission on October 17, 1930, he heard the Gospel preached in its beauty and power for the first time in many years. A sudden realization of sin overcame Woysch. All night long he wrestled in turmoil of soul. That next night, October 18, found him in the mission a second time, now in full contrition, accepting Jesus Christ as Savior. His preaching now is not a mockery; it is a heartfelt experience.

The present pastor of Glenwood, Illinois, United Church was reborn in Pacific Garden Mission hardly ten years ago. Arthur E. Petznick had run away from home at the age of twenty, finally securing employment in Detroit until the depression. Loss of work, gambling, life in the Chicago slums followed in quick turn. Grant Park benches were his bed many times. On October 9, 1931, as the police entered the front door of a pool-room at State and Harrison, the quickest exit for Petznick was a side door. Walking down State street on this cold, rainy day he welcomed the invitation of a worker at the mission door. The first thing that attracted him inside the hall was the sign, HOW LONG SINCE YOU WROTE TO MOTHER? Suddenly he realized what a disgrace he was to his home; when Dad Taylor preached, he realized what a disgrace he was in the sight of God. In the prayer room that

night he made place in his heart for Christ. A course at the
Moody Bible Institute followed. Now, with his wife, Arthur E.
Petznick is testifying to the saving power of God in full-time
Christian service.

"I shudder to think that I might now be filling a drunkard's
grave," says Edson H. Minor, "were it not for that God-blessed
lighthouse." Minor went smoothly through Sunday school and
his home church until he became a travelling salesman and
became a drink addict. Then he married a Southern girl,
hoping that her Christian influence would help him master the
habit. It was to no avail; he lost job after job, until all friends
and relatives turned from him but his praying wife. But in
1926 his wife said she was returning to her own people in the
South, until Minor had a life-changing experience. Thereupon
Minor began to drift with the homeless, jobless, friendless tide
on State Street, and one night he walked into the mission. He
went out and resisted God for three weeks, afraid to surrender
his life, afraid of what others would say, afraid to give up the
liquor habit. On Sunday night, July 19, 1936, he found it impossible to resist the urge to go to the old mission, and there
accepted the saving work of Christ. "I found joy, peace, hap-
piness, friends — but most of all, forgiveness in Christ," he
told the mission circle. "I soon had a good position and my
dear wife came back to a home where Jesus is Head of the
house."

William James Taylor, alias Bill Hennessy, alias Ed Lynch,
alias Tom O'Brien and whatever other appellation was expedient
and helpful, learned that he couldn't hide from God. At the age
of three, behind his father's San Francisco saloon he grew into
a taste for liquor by dipping his baby fingers into the dregs of
glasses and bottles. Small wonder that by twelve he was a
drunken street urchin. After two years in a reform school he
lived aimlessly until a second arrest placed him in an industrial
institution. Gambling, drugs and drink both provided a liveli-
hood and made him a constant fugitive from the law that kept
him constantly on the move, whenever he wasn't serving sentence.
The night he arrived in Chicago, he hurried into Pacific Garden
Mission to avoid what he thought were suspicious glances of a
policeman. He returned a second night. Again he heard the
testimonies of what God had done for such as he. Walking to
the front, he knelt at the altar and repeated after the personal
worker, "God be merciful to me, a sinner, and save me now
for Jesus' sake." "That night," Taylor said, "I slept in a bed

and took my shoes off my feet, which had not been done for
some time. And since then I haven't used any drugs, nor
have I wanted any. I cannot tell all Jesus Christ has done for
me. But one thing I can do, and that is tell others about Him.
And there's a lot of things I don't know. But there's one thing
I do know. And that is God ain't any picker of persons."

Of such was the Kingdom built as Ma and Dad Taylor worked
loyally under divine empowerment. Although his own testimony
was not spectacular in the sense of what many others at the mission could give, nevertheless Taylor's ministry was powerful.
He was a full-fledged preacher; the seven or eight heavily marked
Bibles in his use attested the fact of his feeding on the Word.

In addition to what the mission could do in the way of providing physical nourishment, secondary, of course, to the evangelistic basis of the work, the mission had its annual Christmas
dinner, inaugurated by Dad Taylor. There was even plum
pudding. The tense moment of excitement came when the first
of the many unsuspecting guests jumped to his feet with the
shout. "Hey, Mr. Taylor, I got a quarter!" It was the cue for
each one to hunt the nickels, dimes, and quarters that Pa had
buried in the dessert. One year, however, the basement, in need
of repairs, could not be utilized for the holiday treat. Dad
Taylor found a solution. Facing the men that Saturday night
before Christmas he said, "Gentlemen, it's near Christmas dinner.
We have $100 in the safe over there. The money was given by
Jesus. We trust you, and Jesus doesn't want you to use it for
snifters. Each of you will receive fifty cents to buy your Christmas dinner." The following Sunday morning revealed what an
unregenerate heart and a crowbar can do. The safe was empty.
Friends made up the necessary amount, however, and the men
had their Christmas dinner.

And he loved these men, ragged in soul. As they found Christ
and gave testimony to His grace, Dad Taylor already anticipated
eagerly the first spiritual birthday of each one. It was something of a principle and tradition with him that no convert speak
from the platform until he was a year old. And there were many
birthday candles that shone with increasing light as the years
cast lengthened beams into this world's night. Twenty-seven was
the largest ingathering of a single night on the State street location during those years. And in the year of 1933 a total of 775
had knelt in prayer at the mission altar. Each one had been
dealt with personally, each one had been given a portion of

Scripture, and each one had professed Christ. That was but one year out of many. Such harvest was both provocative and indicative of Dad Taylor's prayer, "To be a piece of machinery at the Holy Spirit's beck and call."

## Chapter XVIII

# THE MAN WHO HEARD GOD LAUGH

But his mother prayed.

Through the years of frolicsome laughter and irresponsible pleasure, this sober fact was the only touch of solemnity that ever brushed the life of Walter R. MacDonald. "Making the other fellow laugh seemed to come as second nature to me even when I was very young," says MacDonald. "So my aim was the stage. I thought that if I could ever have my name in marquee lights for the public to gaze upon, that would be the height of my ambition."

That goal was reached. A veteran entertainer who for more than thirty-seven years had sparked hollow laughter into empty hearts encouraged the lad's interests. Before many months had passed Walter was on the upper side of the bright lights. It offered a gay crowd, this vaudeville and stage business. And a good fellow couldn't refuse an occasional drink. So the proverbial camel had wedged his nose into MacDonald's life: more and more, whiskey became an actual threat to the entertainer's success. At the end of 1924 came the beginning of a six-months' drunk. During this time he was playing with one of America's leading comedians who told MacDonald that the top of the ladder was easily his if wild life and whiskey stepped out. But already there was no more shaking of this awful vise of drink.

Several months later the switchboard operator, a pretty little thing, at the Illinois Masonic Hospital where MacDonald was visiting a friend, said, quite startlingly, "Sir, I don't know of any doctor who can help you, but I do know of Someone else who can." There was no asking what she meant; the tiny office couldn't very well conceal a drunkard's breath. "What is his name, and what is his address?" was MacDonald's reply. "His name is Jesus, and His address is Heaven," said Miss Alberta Schultz, who only a year previous had found Christ. She wasn't ashamed of the New Testament on her desk, either. He asked her out; she asked him in—to Pacific Garden Mission, her spiritual birthplace.

Together they attended Pacific Garden Mission meetings for several weeks. Then MacDonald hurried away to fill his engagements as entertainer. Queer evenings they were: an appetizer of Gospel singing, testimonies and preaching, followed by a diet of comedy and error. For five weeks Mac-Donald continued in this manner, entranced by the powerful singing, varied music, witnesses and Gospel messages, and then swallowed by the whirl of night revelry. Laughter was still coming MacDonald's way.

One night Pa Taylor shifted the scene. MacDonald was booked to entertain a lodge that evening. Since it was too early for his act, he wandered into the mission. Already under the influence of liquor, MacDonald propped a hymnal under each arm to hide the trembling of his alcohol-wracked body. Thus he sat, inwardly feasting on what he heard, and admiring again the forceful, unabashed words of Superintendent Taylor. This was the second week after the Taylors' return from a vacation. Although the preaching the three previous weeks had been excellent, there was something about this man's sermons which came from the very God Himself. MacDonald listened, and winced as the misshapen tip of the preacher's crooked index finger seemed to veer constantly in his direction.

### PSALM I

Blessed is the man that walketh not in the counsel of the ungodly, nor standeth in the way of sinners, nor sitteth in the seat of the scornful.

But his delight is in the law of the Lord; and in his law doth he meditate day and night.

And he shall be like a tree planted by the rivers of water, that bringeth forth his fruit in his season; his leaf also shall not wither; and whatsoever he doeth shall prosper.

The ungodly are not so: but are like the chaff which the wind driveth away.

Therefore the ungodly shall not stand in the judgment, nor sinners in the congregation of the righteous.

For the Lord knoweth the way of the righteous: but the way of the ungodly shall perish.

It was the Scripture reading for that night, supplemented by these words, unnerving to the gay MacDonald: "He that sitteth in the heavens shall laugh" (Ps. 2:4). Then followed the full-toned voice of Taylor as he interpreted how God's laughter might sound. And there was the accusing crooked finger again coupled with the repetition: "He that sitteth in the heavens shall laugh." Strange, thought MacDonald, that God or a preacher or conversion could have any joy and laughter. That was the very thing he had always feared: the loss of laughter. That was why MacDonald was gayer than ever that night, staging his act and drinking his health. Nevertheless Taylor's laugh stuck, and those shattering words of Psalm 2:4, "He that sitteth in the heavens shall laugh."

Despite the upsetting message of the previous evening, MacDonald returned to Pacific Garden Mission the next night, May 29, 1925. It was the first time he failed to fill his engagement as entertainer. Instead, when the Gospel invitation was given, MacDonald was on his knees before God, uttering a penitent's prayer and a sinner's need of Jesus Christ.

It was MacDonald who first called the Taylors "Pa" and "Ma." It was a mark of true love, growing from the realization that Pa Taylor, instead of being "hard on him" as Walter complained to Mrs. Taylor, was seeking to ground this new convert in the faith and in a dedication of talent to God. For two years MacDonald worked at the mission, using his excellent voice, song-leading ability, laughter and testimony for God's glory. Meanwhile he learned, too, that Pa was right in saying, "You're not worth your salt unless you read the Bible and pray."

For the occasion of his first anniversary at Pacific Garden Mission, MacDonald brought his parents and younger brother from Detroit. That night became brother Roy's spiritual birthday. Later Walter had the joy of leading other family members to Christ.

Seven years as song leader followed, before Walter MacDonald entered independent evangelistic preaching. So great is his testimony and work for Christ, and so multitudinous the harvest of souls throughout the United States and Canada that when Pacific Garden Mission asked its son to participate in the sixty-fifth anniversary celebration, it was two years late. Walter MacDonald is booked for meetings that far in advance. Fortunately, however, rearrangements in schedule permitted the Pacific Garden family to see and hear this great soul-winning evangelist. Walter MacDonald is no longer the prancer; his feet are grounded on the Rock Christ Jesus.

## Chapter XIX

## TRIMMING THE LOWER LIGHTS

Unique from his birthday, Harry George Saulnier has held his own place in the world from the day two hospital nurses inadvertently exchanged him with another baby, a mistake his mother immediately rectified. Born in a sector of the Bronx where respectable people with moderate incomes reside, Harry weighed ten pounds at birth. He began preaching the first night, August 19, 1902.

Harry's parents were French born. His father, a linguist and French army officer, came from Calais; his mother, who had realized the dream of every girl's heart, to travel around the world in the employ of a wealthy family, came from Chaumont. New York, rather than native France, was their meeting place, and there they married.

As a lad Saulnier was supershy. Introductions and company frightened him; even calls from family friends sent him scurrying into closets. Nor did Christian and Missionary Alliance boys' camp with other eight-year-olds remedy the situation. There was one Person, however, that he longed to know better, but nobody seemed to help him. His father quite often knelt beside his bed for prayer, but never spoke to Harry about his soul; his various Sunday school teachers taught the weekly lesson, but when Harry asked who Jesus was, never answered quite satisfactorily; preachers of several denominations never seemed to give a personal invitation while he was present. Night after night he stopped for a street meeting in Fordham Square, where a group gave testimonies and distributed Gospel portions. He carefully gathered the New Testament library of twenty-seven books. But no one ever talked personally with Harry about his soul.

After finishing high school, Harry went to work as a sign company electrician, sending many of Broadway's white lights into their initial flare. Once while connecting a huge sign for the Black Cat Restaurant in Greenwich Village, all the fastenings but one bolt tore loose from the bricks. Dangling in midair with the thousand pound sign, Saulnier knew that if the other fastener gave way, there was no alternative to a crushing death. The bolt held.

The enthusiasm of his oldest sister who moved to Chicago was so great that another sister and finally the entire family followed suit. That included Harry, who immediately branded Chicago the dirtiest city in the country. Going to work with the Commonwealth Edison Company as electrician, he maintained employment there until 1940 when, after a unique record of Christian service, he felt impelled to accept the superintendency of Pacific Garden Mission. Under his leadership the mission has stilted to its present big-time program and is successfully multiplying the work of its earlier epochs.

Saulnier found salvation on August 21, 1925, having passed as a Christian for several years. Two years before his conversion, he had been elected president of the Christian Endeavor unit at the Edgewater Presbyterian Church, of which he was a member; the following year he headed the entire north shore division of Christian Endeavor. There was no doubt about his popularity, enhanced very likely by his proud possession of a Model T Ford. And he suffered the customary throes of adolescent love, to his educational enrichment, if not, fortunately, to premature entanglements. He never drank, smoked or danced; movies were his only weakness. Then came news that his father, who was visiting a brother in Italy, died there. And his sisters had shortly before moved from Chicago. That incomparably cruel loneliness of a big city was upon him. Quite perplexed, Saulnier turned to his Bible. From its pages gleamed the words of II Timothy 2: 4, and he readily confessed that he was "all entangled in the affairs of this life."

That was August 19, his birthday. He came under tremendous conviction and felt he must attend a preaching service somewhere. John Roach Stratton, then pastor of New York's Calvary Baptist Church, was holding a Chicago campaign. Telling his employer it was his birthday, he asked for the afternoon off. The congregation was mostly women and Stratton gave no invitation. Saulnier returned that night; again no appeal for souls was made. The following afternoon he again missed work, but no invitation was given at that service nor at the one in the evening. He went home in desperation and slipped to his knees in prayer. It was almost dawn when he awakened out of sleep, still kneeling at his bedside. Light was streaming through the window, and in Saulnier's heart the light of a new-found joy evidenced his salvation of that night, August 21, 1925.

From that moment he mingled with growing Christians. He spoke in missions and churches and attended prayer meeting regularly. Monday nights he met with a north side fisherman's club, sharing in the testimony meetings and tract distribution. His first street meeting, in Evanston, brought a shower of peas pelted by several young dentists in an overhead office. It was a good corner, however, so the workers continued there undismayed. The following week a well-dressed woman came along, listened to the testimonies, knelt on the street and took Christ as Savior. Then she offered a five dollar bill to the group leader. He smilingly refused it.

Saulnier attended Moody Bible Institute night school for two years, 1926-1928, continuing, meanwhile, as re-elected president of the north shore Christian Endeavor. In June, 1928, he married Gene Beryl Tucker, whom he had met several years before in Endeavor circles. She was a splendid Christian, gave musical readings, and was "the prettiest girl in the whole town." Furthermore, he liked brown—he often wears a brown shirt, brown suit and brown tie to match his brown eyes—and Gene Beryl Tucker had brown hair and brown eyes.

With Saulnier's widening interests, he sensed a gradual growth away from the Christian Endeavor movement. In June, 1928, however, his north shore leadership graduated him into presidency for the whole Chicago area, and he seized the opportunity to incorporate an evangelistically-minded regime into strategic offices. Vic Cory, then with the Bible Institute Colportage Association, became prayer meeting chairman. Caspar Henning, a godly civil engineer, became second vice-president. That triumvirate shook the Chicago units with Christian fervor for two years. The conventions were moved back to Moody Institute, where they had once been held in the days of huge crowds. Registrations broke all previous records. In 1930, when Saulnier's term expired, he remained on the Endeavor cabinet, but sought, meanwhile, a more direct outlet for his evangelistic energies.

Saulnier and Henning became interested in a north side mission on Devon avenue. For a while they assisted the pastor in a general way. When he moved to another field, they bought the equipment and paid the rent. They built a good Sunday school but had no outstanding conversions. There were two reasons. A rescue mission program is seldom effective in a so-called respectable area; furthermore, their mission was on the second floor. After a time the mission moved to the basement of Saulnier's home near the Northside Mission Covenant Church. When the main success was in a growing Sunday school, the leaders merged it with the church effort and became church school teachers there.

Then Harry Saulnier got one of those big ideas which, nurtured in prayer and work, constantly gave him a tremendous reputation in evangelistic circles. In 1932, when still on the Christian Endeavor cabinet, he brought the idea of a citywide Easter Sunrise service before the annual officers' meeting. He had wrestled with the vision for several years; friends said it was impractical. The leaders, however, now called together the advisory board of past presidents and representative pastors to consider the proposition. They decided the Endeavor was too small to make the venture a success. Since the Christian Endeavor units were operative in seven denominations only, which did not include Baptists, Lutherans, Episcopalians, or any of the Swedish, Norwegian or German groups, they voted to approach the Century of Progress evangelistic council, representing all denominations. Two months before Easter, 1933, accordingly, leaders of fifteen big young people's organizations in the city gathered and pledged enthusiastic support. Saulnier was made chairman. Despite an all night threat of rain and a light sprinkle, the service went off satisfactorily, but the downpour, which continued all day, began after the 15,000 worshippers had filed from the stands. The turnout had exceeded all expectations. Hats, tin cans and paper boxes were pressed into service for the offering.

Since then the service has become an annual event in Soldier Field, donated for the purpose by park board authorities. Twice the attendance has exceeded 55,000. Saulnier declared that "if God hadn't sent the sunshine, nobody would ever have come back a second time." His philosophy—"work like the blazes but give God the glory"—has enabled him to gather a corps of talented lay workers who yearly now prod tens of thousands from their homes long before dawn to attend the resurrection day assembly. His reputation as a slave-driver he justifies by asserting "it's the Lord's work." Forty years young, with a gray spangled head of black hair, he effervesces with enthusiasm. He often has little sense of time and space in his crowded, far-flung ministry, and is in perpetual motion.

First contact with the Pacific Garden Mission on Saulnier's part came in 1935 when the rescue house needed another trustee. Caspar Henning, already a member of the board, made the proposal. Saulnier had visited the mission several years before: the place was crowded, Pop Taylor was at his best, and Harry enjoyed it immensely. Soon, at Taylor's request, Harry was speaking thrice a month to the mission crowd on Thursday nights, Dad's night off. He saw a number of converts under his preaching, although none of them had sensational testimonies. He kept his preaching assignment until Dad Taylor retired in 1936, when T. Donald Gately followed as superintendent.

Gately, himself, was an example of leadership that Pacific Garden produced among its converts. Converted there when Bob Ingersoll was superintendent at the Van Buren street location, he maintained an active testimony and interest. Miss Moody, who had been mission pianist and secretary, became Mrs. Gately. When Mr. Taylor, because of physical debility, found it advisable to leave the mission superintendency, T. Donald Gately filled the breach before entering specialized work among children. He served as mission leader for four years.

In those years, Saulnier spent increasingly more time in the mission area. In 1934 it was he who revived the Saturday night street meetings on State and Harrison, and brought a fishermen's group. That corner was the site of his first run-in with the State street toughs. Bartender "Muzzie" was furious at the idea of a church service in the backyard of his corner saloon. First he parked automobiles along the curb, hoping the street preachers would take another corner, but they shoved the cars out of the way. Then "Muzzie" planted men to threaten the car-budgers. One night "Muzzie" foamed out of the tavern, shouting, "Leave your hands off those cars or I'll . . . . ;" and fumed back to wait on his patrons. A newly-acquired loud speaker no longer made the corner site a prerequisite, but "Muzzie" tallied by erecting a like instrument over his tavern door to blare jazz interference. Finally "Muzzie" gave up. When Saulnier said, "Why don't you take Christ as your Savior, Muz?" the bartender had a ready answer: "I'd rather take you for a one-way ride!" Harry chuckled and looked him straight in the eye. "Muzzie," he said, "we're your best friends. We've come right here to your corner, to bring you the Gospel."

When T. Donald Gately resigned the mission superintendency in January, 1940, the trustees had no successor in view, despite the forty candidates. News of the opening had spread to mission men around the country, but the authorities could not agree on any of the possibilities. Gately promised to continue for two months until a successor was found. When February came, however, the call was still unmet and the trustees felt that God had a peculiar answer for the mission's pressing problem. Unable to attend the February board meeting, lawyer Paul Fischer sent a short list of suggestions in the order of preference. At the top of his list stood the name of a fellow board member, Harry Saulnier. It was the first time the possibility had been mentioned, and Saulnier, who was present, was utterly blank-faced. A unanimous call was extended with a week's time for decision. Saulnier and his wife prayed all week. That Friday night she said, "Harry, I think the Lord wants you to say 'yes.'" Somewhat quizzically he answered, "Gene, I feel that way, too." Then he ran to the telephone, called the secretary of the board, and said, "O. K. I'm coming."

## CHAPTER XX

## FOLD OF THE LOST SHEEP

April 1, 1940, was Harry Saulnier's first official day as superintendent. He appeared for work the previous night, pleading with sinners to come to Jesus. That was the night Charlie Mason handed him a loaded .38 calibre pistol which he had stolen from his brother, an Ohio deputy sheriff, to make some holdups.

"Take this gun, before I kill myself or somebody else," said Mason.

The meeting had just ended when Mason entered. All night long he had walked up and down the street in front of the mission, hearing the amplified service. The men had gone to their beds and Saulnier, about to lock up, waved Mason inside. They sat down, alone, in the mission hall. Mason was still carrying his gun in his pocket when Saulnier pulled out a New Testament and began reading from Romans 6.

"I'm saved but I'm a backslider," said the gunman.

"Then let's pray," said Saulnier. As he slid to his knees alongside the old Billy Sunday piano, he added, "First give me that gun." Mason handed it over and they poured out their hearts to God. Six months later the news reached the sheriff's office in Ohio, and Mason's brother scribbled a note to Saulnier, asking him to send the pistol. "It is a pleasure," wrote Saulnier.

During these ten years of Saulnier's superintendency, the converts have come from every walk of life. The primary emphasis, however, is still to salvage the outcast. The presentation of the invitation to Jesus has changed somewhat, for Saulnier knows that "Mother's prayers seldom follow wayward sons in this generation; in fact, many mothers are worse than their children." So it is a direct appeal to come to the Lamb of God which taketh away the sin of the world, that Saulnier gives. The crowd is asked to bow in prayer; then the superintendent usually repeats that great invitation, "Come unto Me, all ye that labor and are heavy laden, and I will give you rest," spoken by Jesus. Then,

*Revised with additions in May, 1950

> Ah, soul, are you here
> Without comfort or rest,
> Marching down the rough pathway of time?
> Make Jesus your friend
> Ere the shadows grow dark
> Oh, accept this sweet peace so sublime.

"How many here tonight would like to take Christ as their Saviour? Raise your hand and give us the blessed privilege of remembering you in prayer."

What hands have been raised in response! Hands of murderers, drunkards, prostitutes, gamblers, adulterers, gigolos, revelers. But other hands, too: hands of musicians, college students, soldiers, sailors and white-collar workers.

"Now that you've given us the privilege of praying *for* you," adds Saulnier, ever pouring out his heart in intercession, "give us the privilege of praying *with* you. Come to the prayer room, while we sing the familiar invitation hymn, 'Just As I Am.' " The Hammond organ resounds, spiritual electricity charges the air, and the penitents start forward as the crowd takes up the words:

> Just as I am, without one plea,
> But that Thy blood was shed for me,
> And that Thou bidd'st me come to Thee,
> O Lamb of God, I come! I come!

Personal workers are going through the audience to see if any are on the verge of decision and need just a word of encouragement. They accompany such to the prayer room, rather than to the front of the main auditorium, for it is quieter and more private.

It is a great heart that beats beneath the vest of the 220-pound, six-foot, three-inch mission overseer. The secret of Saulnier's success is his deep personal interest in other people. He numbers among his personal friends such workers as William R. Newell, Walter L. Wilson, William L. Pettingill, William McCarrell, J. I. Overholtzer and "Ma" Sunday. He never met Billy personally, although he heard him a number of times, but "Ma" Sunday says that "Billy would be delighted in Harry's conduct of the mission." Once she volunteered, "Dad would be one-hundred percent for a man who loves souls like that."

Right there she placed her finger on the bright spot of Saulnier's superintendency. More than four hundred converts a month, on an average, are being made at the State Street lighthouse. Many a church would delight in a record of a hundred converts a year, but in 1949 Saulnier's records show 7,577 persons, representing every state in the Union, won to Christ. Twenty-eight hundred and ninety-one of these were servicemen, and were won to Christ by faithful workers in the Servicemen's Center.

An efficient staff of workers gets much credit from Saulnier. His assistants are John Huffman and U. S. Grant Sension. Other workers include Dennis Snell, personal worker; Mrs. Karl Jensen, secretary; Miss Laurine Johnson, bookkeeper; Ben Engstrom, building superintendent; Ervin Maus, assistant building superintendent; Edward G. Sale, Charles Schneider, Grant Holycross, doormen; Clarence Renn, night supervisor; Leonard Tunelius, cook; Hannibal Washington, file clerk.

Behind the scenes, directing the business activities of the Mission, are the trustees. Both professional and businessmen, they are all men with a burden for lost souls. Thomas S. Smith, "the Apple King of the Midwest" and father of author Dr. Wilbur M. Smith, is president of the trustees. Other trustees, besides Superintendent Saulnier, are: Freelin A. Carlton, vice president, department store manager; Caspar F. Henning, secretary, civil engineer, Fire Insurance; Roy Baumann, treasurer, home appliance dealer; William W. Gothard, assistant secretary. executive director, Gideons International; J. Paul Bennett, M. D., assistant treasurer, roentgenologist; Victor E. Cory, president of Scripture Press; R. Y. Dantuma, president of Reliance Typesetting Company; John M. Fiddler, G. E. Medical Products Company; William Garland, president of Johnson Glass Company; Walter D. Mishler, sales manager; Frank E. Sandberg, O. D.; and Andrew Wyzenbeek, president of Wyzenbeek Staff.

These men often aid in placing mission converts in business and manufacturing firms, following interviews to determine their qualifications. Workers, with educational backgrounds ranging from a year's grammar school to graduation from Harvard, have been placed in hotels, restaurants, mail order concerns, railroads, machine shops, garages and factories.

Prerequisite to an increase in conversions when Saulnier took over was a step-up in the attendance of down-and-outers. For various reasons the attendance had decreased. As Saulnier burned midnight oil and mingled with the men, showing a genuine love for them, attendance shot up. Less than a year later, more than twice as many were attending services and being ministered to—and conversions more than doubled. Today, attendance at the mission is on the increase again. In 1949, for instance, more than 100,000 heard the Gospel in the mission.

As attendance has increased, the old problem of turnover has become increasingly acute. More than ever the mission has had to drive for decisions among men attending for the first time. There is an efficient follow-up campaign; the converts are put to work, asked to come to prayer meetings and Bible classes, to give their testimonies, and to help with tract distribution.

Saulnier revived noon street meetings five days a week and nightly meetings three times a week at the northwest corner of State and Harrison. Usually he directs the noon meetings and an assistant takes the night sessions. Both old timers and young converts step up to tell their stories. George Snow tells how he used to cheat the suckers in the gambling dens, and how Christ saved him. Successful loop merchants and professional men, Christian businessmen, add their words of testimony to Christ's redemptive power.

Tract work has more than doubled under Saulnier's leadership. Between 200,000 and 250,000 leaflets are distributed annually. Saulnier is a great believer in religious journalism. Wherever he goes—whether by foot, automobile, train or airplane—he distributes a tract or "one of these lovely road maps to heaven": the Gospel of John. During war years a conductor on the Sante Fe, alert for enemy propagandists, became suspicious of Saulnier's tract work. At the next station a plain-clothes detective boarded the train, and, taking a seat next to Saulnier, struck up a conversation. Soon Saulnier gave him a printed folder and told him about the Lord. "I'm a good Methodist!" blurted the detective.

"That's all right," answered Saulnier. "You've got to be born again, too."

In February 1941, PG inaugurated a women's work, supervised by Mrs. Susan Wymer, jail and mission worker. The new department began to make converts and became an integral part of the mission, taking over its jail visitation among women. Heading the Ladies' Auxiliary is Mrs. Leta Jacobson. Miss Ida Robinson is matron of the women's dormitory where beds are provided. Through arrangement with authorities in the Women's Court in the Central Police Station, delinquent girls have been sent to the mission for shelter and vocational guidance. The Traveler's Aid Society, Red Cross and Salvation Army also direct to the mission young girls and mothers who drift into Chicago.

When blonde Betty Alvis set out from Alabama for Wisconsin in her early twenties, she felt that a job would soon offset any lonliness, but she was wrong. A truck driver offered her a ride to Chicago and she accepted, but she lost her pocket book and all her belongings except the slack suit in which she was garbed, in a struggle in which she saved her honor. Chicago police picked her up sleeping on the Windy City streets. During the Sunday afternoon jail service by the mission women she accepted Christ. When her case was heard in court, the presiding magistrate asked whether anyone would help her. "The missionary at Pacific Garden Mission," she answered. The mission telephone rang, and soon Betty was escorted to the women's dormitory. The same night, with the glow of Christian testimony on her face, she boarded a bus for Alabama. There she has carried on a splendid work among young people in her community, and has walked the marriage aisle with a saved companion, with whom she has established a Christian home.

Another visitor who will long be remembered by workers of the Women's Division is Norma Lee Browning. Dressed in her short yellow dress, shabby red coat and shoes, she melted quite naturally into the patchwork of neon lights and gaudy shop fronts. In a sense she was privileged, however, for in her pocket she guarded a note of introduction to the Women's Division.

Approaching the door with its caption, "Free Friendly Service to Women," she, of course, became aware of other things. The most stupendous object, and the most shocking and overpowering, was the huge red and gold neon illuminated sign "Christ Died for Our Sins" topping the emblem of the cross with its "Jesus Saves," and underneath, "Pacific Garden Mission."

Norma would not know, of course, that this 35-foot sign was dedicated on Oct. 5, 1948, as a memorial to Walter G. (Pop) Taylor. Nor would she realize its cost of $3500. What she saw, and what no one could fail to see, was the startling message of Jesus' love—startling not because of its fact, but startling because of its insistent domination and invitation over and above and in the midst of the Row's hell gates.

Compelling, too, were the strains of a hymn pouring from the mission hall's loud-speaker. The cacophony of street cars, automobiles, elevated trains, and the felt, rather than heard restlessness of shuffling, stumbling, searching feet were overruled by the Gospel song.

But it was lodging she wanted! The gray-haired matron of the women's dormitory led her to the nine-bed room, and indicated a clean, neat place of rest. Norma admitted hunger, too, and offered the ability to buy a meal, a cheap one, that is. But here the matron was graciously helpful also: she herself offered to cook a warm meal for the transient girl, and later to help her find work.

Norma asked about the Gospel meeting and soon slipped unobtrusively into a back row of the hall. Men were giving testimonies —to salvation in Christ Jesus; to friendships found; to rescue from sin—all through the ministry and loving compassion of those in the Pacific Garden Mission. The hungry girl in the shabby clothes listened, watched, remembered.

Slipping away unseen after the service she escaped into the maze of the engulfing city. Shortly thereafter, on Dec. 4, 1949, The Chicago *Tribune* carried a convincing front-page feature story by one of its reporters, Norma Lee Browning!

Taking to the air at the invitation of Radio Station WMBI, the mission at first broadcast its Saturday night service every other week from May to August. At present, broadcasts are heard on the first Monday morning of every month. One of Saulnier's objectives is a daily broadcast from the mission which lacks but two essentials: a radio station that will donate the time on the air, and a sponsor to pay the monthly rental for a wire to the mission.

So vigorously has the mission grown that present facilities have become overtaxed and inadequate. The present auditorium seats slightly more than two hundred, and often at noon-day meetings is crowded beyond capacity. The present dormitory, accommodating 85, is overcrowded and often men have had to be turned out into a winter night to tramp through the snow without lodging. Staff members and friends are praying for an additional building to provide the necessary space for proper conduct of the work.

Expansion in the last decade has been steady. Inspired by a God-given vision, the trustees in July 1941 made the first payment on a $30,000 purchase price for the two buildings just north of the mission. The first practical outgrowth of this move was the dedication on Nov. 29, 1942, of a new Christian Servicemen's Center, with a chapel seating 150, a lounge, a library and writing room, a recreation and game room, and canteen. Interested Christians furnished the funds, mostly in small gifts, and this coupled, with a $16,000 endowment met the cost of the buildings, decorations and furnishings, the complete undertaking being a faith venture of $45,000. During 1943 the dormitory equipped with fifty beds was completed at a cost of $8,000.

Since its dedication during the war years the Servicemen's Center has remained open to young men in khaki and blue, men eager to spend a few free hours in the Windy City and not certain where to go. State Street offers them cheap restaurants, taverns, shooting galleries, burlesque theaters and everything else under the sun. As the soldiers and sailors walk by the center, the doorman says, "C'mon inside for hot coffee and sandwiches, fellows. It's free. This is a servicemen's center. Don't cost you a cent."

During the first month the Servicemen's Center was open, fifty men confessed Christ. One night a private and a lieutenant knelt together and gave their lives to Jesus. The second month the number doubled. In February, the third month, there were 150, and March records showed that an added 398 soldiers and sailors had come to Christ. Claude Bulander, personal work director at the time, himself had 18 converts, and the decisions totaled 40 on April 1; it was "April Fool's Day for the devil," the staff remarked. By the end of the first six months 25,000 men in uniform had visited the new haven. They wore uniforms of almost all the allied nations taking a significant part in the global struggle. They reported having seen action in Australia, New Zealand, North Africa—almost every fighting front being represented. One lad, asked about his address, said, "Put me down for Casa Blanca." Estimated attendance figures over eight years show that nearly a half million have visited the Center, with some 30,000 decisions for Christ. The servicemen's dormitory today furnishes 45 beds for service personnel, and continues to do a booming business, especially on week ends. The mission provides a free breakfast, at which as many as five men have given their first testimony on a single occasion, after having been led to Christ the previous night.

While the Center is a happy host to Christian servicemen, its outreach to others is what makes it supremely a Christian Center. Its two-fold purpose is to provide a recreation center with a Christian atmosphere for all servicemen regardless of creed or color, and to furnish a missionary center where men in uniform can be helped with their spiritual problems. Located near four railroad stations serving Chicago, the Center is visited daily by scores of men who have an hour to spend before their trains leave. Actively assisting Harry G. Saulner the director, are Edward H. Ockert, director of personal work and his assistant Otto Hintz. Scores of volunteer personal workers, including Mr. and Mrs. Claude Bulander, Arthur Brown, Peter Potkonjak, Charles Clohsey and Ralph Osterloo, spend many hours every week reaching servicemen for Christ. Miss Norma Greenwell, as head receptionist, supervises the reception desk with its many-sided responsibilities, while Miss Dorothy Reichenbach, as canteen supervisor, makes sure that every serviceman has plenty to eat.

The Servicemen's Center, like the work among the men and women of Skid Row, is made possible by gifts from God's people. However, Christians have come personally to lift the load. During its early months young people's groups from many Chicago churches assisted with maintenance and paid for a part of the furnishings. Later, women's societies from various Chicago churches pitched in regularly, and even today help from time to time providing and serving refreshments. The evangelistic program has always been carried on in a tactful, unoffensive manner, but is remarkably effective.

A Christian brakeman on the Great Northern, on the Fargo, North Dakota, to Minneapolis, Minnesota run has been a real friend of the Center. He keeps copies of *A Doorway to Heaven* on the train for distribution to Chicago-bound servicemen. Not infrequently the uniformed men come to the mission and then to the Servicemen's Center, where the Gospel is proclaimed to them.

Long before the Servicemen's Center opened, the old mission proved to be God's U.S.O. for many a man called to the colors. One of these was Bob Neilson, "the happiest sailor in the Navy." Bob joined the Navy in February 1942, and on Memorial Day was bound down State Street in a streetcar. He jumped off a half block from the mission and wandered inside. "Well," he says, "I was saved at 9:40 P.M. Thank God I didn't get back to my station the way some of the others did. It was like a nightmare to see them, and to remember that I had been like that too. I'm the happiest sailor in the Navy!" Bob saw five transports go down off Africa and, inside of a few months, led 19 fellow sailors to a personal trust in Christ. Then he wrote the mission: "I'm still the happiest sailor in the Navy. Praise God for that wonderful night at P.G. God already has rewarded me with 19 souls."

The story of Bob Neilson, now a pastor in the Philadelphia area, has been told to thousands, having originally appeared in the *Pacific Garden Mission News,* a monthly publication launched in 1936. Today Christians in every state and many foreign countries read the *News,* and find it a source of encouragement and inspiration. One invalid man in Asheville, N. C., reads the *News* in order to pray for specific needs (every evening at 7 o'clock he prays for the mission, despite the fact he has never visited Chicago). The *News,* a four-page, attractively designed publication, is mailed free of charge to anyone requesting it. Since 1948 James R. Adair, editor of *Power* and *My Counsellor,* nationally known Sunday School papers, has edited the *News,* and Edwin Pike has been art editor.

Another important phase of the mission program today is "Out of the Night," the mission's 16 mm. sound and color documentary film. With more than 150 prints of the film in circulation over the country, literally hundreds have professed Christ as personal Saviour after witnessing the power of the Gospel in action on Skid Row.

David Saulnier, son of the superintendent, supervises the mission's film department which handles all details in connection with the renting and leasing of "Out of the Night." Assisting him are Miss Shirley Rodgers, secretary, and Dan Kearney, clerk.

While "Out of the Night" gives a graphic account of the battle the Pacific Garden Mission is waging against sin on the southern fringe of the Loop, one must visit the area to get the full significance of the deplorable conditions that exist there.

On all sides are doors where men and women check their consciences as they enter. Cheap hotels are headquarters for prostitutes; procurers lounge in drinking dives to enlist customers.

Burlesque houses continue to display gaudy signs of women in the nude, at which passersby halt to avidly anticipate the pleasures of the stage unfrocking inside. The sex centers were given a setback a few years ago when the Chicago *Daily Times* ridiculed Mayor Kelly's closing the Selwyn Theater where "Tobacco Road" was playing, because it was a "mass of obscenity." The *Times* quoted a police sergeant as stating that while "Tobacco Road" broke seven of the ten commandments, strip teasers in the burlesque houses out did that.

The once beautiful but now weatherbeaten chorines pour into skintight gowns, only to shed them again with gestures, wriggles, wobbles, twists and squirms, to the catcalls and whistles of delighted moronic sex-perverts who infest the audience. Nervously shifting in their seats, and watching with glassy eyes, are a good sprinkling of youngsters who hardly know the full significance of it all, but who are getting a post-graduate sex education overnight. There are plenty of old men, so wrecked from sin that the only thrills they can find are lewd jokes and suggestive dances. Then there are ladies (if one may be that charitable) who loudly laugh, cackle and bray as hammy comedians waste time between the performers' scanty change of scenery.

It is a fifty-minute show, during which debased beauty makes sex a target of vile slurs and obscenity. The "girl choruses" feature painted has-beens who double at shedding flimsy garments. Their lurid dances, their routine of sexy filth, stimulate the emotions of patrons and make them enthusiastic visitors at the near-by taverns, dance halls, recreation parlors and other dens. During the burlesque intermission, a hawker sells the sex-starved clientele French postcards at a nickel each.

Outside, the stench of perspiring hot dogs, the swing music of cabaret bands, the parade of unmasked hell itself merge into a caterwaul of depraved humanity. Here is where the mission has deliberately chosen to prove its mettle. There is no running away from sin. Rather, sheathed in the full armor of God, its testimony plucks the fiery darts of Satan from many a pierced target. It is a struggle against mighty forces, as David Anderson, in the November 17, 1940 edition of the Chicago *Tribune*, writes:

> Competition is tough on South State street, but the old Pacific Garden Mission still does a thriving business in men's souls.
> Night and day thousands of homeless men—bums, hoboes in from the wheat fields, ragged pan-handlers, crippled up, mumbling, shuffling men—limp down South State street from Van Buren to 11th street and then plod back again. It's a parade of perpetual motion second only to West Madison street. Where they go, whence they come, is nobody's business and nobody cares much.
> Under the gaudy marquees of the burlesque shows they stop to look

at the posters of hefty blondes. Or, they gather at the open doors
of the tatoo parlors and watch the artist tatoo a spread eagle on the
chest of a sailor. Sometimes as they move past the barber shops
they wink at the lady barbers.

Each night the mission houses 73 men on iron cots upstairs after
the services on the main floor are over. The men bring bundles of
newspapers for bedding. Some evenings as many as 200 persons
crowd into the hall to hear the singing and preaching. Harry G.
Saulnier, superintendent, estimates that in a single month the mission
has managed to find a job for 20 to 30 men. "But we don't keep
record of such things," he adds.

"Our first work," he says, "is the saving of souls. Giving men
a place to sleep and finding jobs is incidental. Bringing men to God
is our primary business. All else is secondary."

With a record of some 50,000 souls, excluding the more than
30,000 servicemen won for Christ in the Servicemen's Center, in
a history three-quarters of a century long, Pacific Garden Mission
continues to hold an unusual place of service in God's Kingdom.
It is one of the 500 missions dotting the United States and Canada.
Usually these centers are classed into four types: 1) the pure Gospel,
which accepts as the motivating basis that the Gospel alone will
do the work; if a man be changed spiritually, all other factors and
relationships will be changed; 2) the community mission, usually
established in poorer districts, which incorporates and promotes all the
various activities of the average church; 3) the welfare mission,
stressing social service as well as spiritual preaching; 4) the industrial
mission which seeks to reach men spiritually by working with them
in manual activities. It is interesting to note that all these classes of
missions also maintain a program of jail work, realizing the need
of help to the outcast as well as to the downcast.

"Houses of miracles" is no misnomer for these help-stations. Each
year thousands of men, women and children, representing as many
thousands of backgrounds, problems, and needs, have been reclaimed
and reclassified.

These missions have varied histories. Some have no specific
denominational affiliation or support, whereas others do; some are
municipally governed, others bear the names of founding individuals
or families; others, again, indicate specialized work among certain
races or creeds.

With the advance in responsibilities and complications of modern
living, methods and means of service are constantly enlarging.
Where once a well-shod worker ministered to a particular area, the

horse-drawn vehicle, then the automobile, and now involved amplification and sound systems bear the same news of salvation. The driving principle seems to be to send the Good News in the quickest way to the most people in the widest area.

Statistics never tell a complete story. They nevertheless, like an arrow, point to a more vital source of illumination. It may be of interest, then, to study the following figures, which represent the partial work from January through April 1950, at Pacific Garden Mission, only one of these 500 "churches in overalls": CONVERSIONS, 1,797; MEALS, 35,830; SLEEPERS, 10,290; ATTEDANCE, 53,025.

Yet basically, these items are but echoes of the greater call to sound the invitation of Him who said:

> "I am the Door; by Me if any man enter in, he shall be saved and shall go in and out, and find pasture.
> "I am the Good Shepherd: the Good Shepherd giveth his life for the sheep.
> "I am the Good Shepherd and know My sheep and am known of Mine.
> "And other sheep I have which are not of this fold: them also I must bring and they shall hear My voice; and there shall be one fold, and one Shepherd."